D0471330

ANDREW JACKSON
1767-1845

Chronology-Documents-Bibliographical Aids

Edited by
RONALD E. SHAW
Professor of History
Miami University

Series Editor
HOWARD F. BREMER

1969
OCEANA PUBLICATIONS, INC.
Dobbs Ferry, New York

Library of Congress Catalog Card Number: 71-83748
Standard Book Number: 379-12063-1

Manufactured in the United States of America

CONTENTS

EDITOR'S FOREWORD

Historians have given the name of Andrew Jackson to an era in the American past. He was one of the most dominant personalities in the American presidency and Jacksonian Democracy has long been recognized as a major phase in American political and social development. Beyond these simple statements, however, there has been little historical agreement about Jackson or his party.

Judgment on Jackson's presidency has undergone constant revision. His party has been variously described as the party of western farmers, eastern workingmen, rising businessmen, reformers and slave owners. It is a mark of the breadth of Jackson's appeal to Americans of his age and of our own that so many schools of interpretation have emerged about Jackson and Jacksonians. These often contradictory interpretations can help us to understand more fully the outstanding issues of Jackson's presidency, such as his contest with South Carolina on the nullification of the tariff, his views on national internal improvements, his conflict with the Second Bank of the United States, the removal of the Indians to the west of the Mississippi River, and in foreign affairs, the settlement of the spoliation claims against France.

This little volume sketches the chronology of Andrew Jackson's life, includes portions of his addresses and messages, and surveys the historical literature written about his presidency. One document which might well have been included here, Jackson's Farewell Address, has been omitted because of its length. The documents in this volume have been taken from James D. Richardson, ed., *Messages and Papers of the Presidents,* Volumes II (Washington, 1897) and III.

CHRONOLOGY

YOUTH IN THE CAROLINAS

1767

March 15   Born: Waxhaw settlement, South Carolina. Father: Andrew; Mother, Elizabeth Hutchinson.

March   Death of his father, shortly before birth of Andrew Jackson.

1774

Attended school of Mr. Branch.

1776

Attended school of Mr. William Humphries.

1779

March 22   Date of oldest document in Jackson MSS in the Library of Congress, a memorandum on cock fighting; but not in Jackson's handwriting.

1780

July   At age 13 joined Major Davies' dragoons on American side in the Revolutionary War and was made a mounted orderly and messenger.

August 6   Witnessed Battle of Hanging Rock, S.C.

1781

April 10   Captured with his brother, Robert, by British dragoons. Slashed by officer's sword when he refused to clean the officer's boots. Held prisoner at Camden, S.C., and became infected with small-pox. The brothers were freed in a prisoner exchange, but Robert died soon after.

November   Orphaned at the death of his mother who was nursing American prisoners in Charleston.

1

1782

Apprenticed to a saddler for six months.

1783

March   Inherited a legacy of more than 300 pounds sterling from Hugh Jackson, in Ireland.

1784

Taught school in Waxhaw settlement.

1785

Read law with Spruce Macay in Salisbury, N.C.

1787

September 26   Admitted to the bar in the itinerant court at Wadesborough, Anson County, North Carolina, and settled in Martinsville.

November 12   Authorized to practice law in the court at Salisbury, Surry County, North Carolina.

TENNESSEE LAWYER AND PLANTER

1788

October   Traveled over the newly opened Cumberland Road to Nashville.

November   Appointed public prosecutor (attorney-general) for the Western District of North Carolina. Boarded with widow of Colonel John Donelson.

1789

November   Journeyed to Natchez, bought land and established trading post on Bayou Pierre north of the settlement.

1790

March   Returned to Nashville.

December 15   Named Attorney General of Mero District of the Territory South of the Ohio River. Commission issued by Governor William Blount, February 15, 1791.

1791

August   Married Rachel Donelson Robards, daughter of Colonel John Donelson, near Natchez.

1794

January 17   A second marriage ceremony performed with Rachel because at the time of the first ceremony her divorce from Lewis Robards had not yet been granted.

1795

Purchased plantation called Hunter's Hill on the Cumberland River near Nashville and established a trading store. Later bought the Hermitage, a plantation three miles northeast of Nashville. Other stores were later established at Gallatin and Lebanon.

1796

January   Delegate to the Tennessee constitutional convention at Knoxville.

December 5   Took seat in the House of Representatives after election as first Representative from Tennessee.

December 5   One of twelve Representatives in the House to vote against a reply giving approval to Washington's Farewell Address.

1797

May   Retired to the life of a planter at Hunter's Hill.

November 22   Took seat in U.S. Senate in Philadelphia, after election as Senator from Tennessee.

1798

April   Resigned from the Senate to deal with personal financial affairs and returned to Tennessee.

October   Appointed judge of the Superior Court (Supreme Court) in Tennessee.

1801

Earliest record of Jackson's membership as a Free Mason.

1802

February   Elected Major General of Tennessee militia.

October 15   Altercation and attempted duel with John Sevier over land frauds and Sevier's disparagement of Jackson's marriage.

1804

March   Became guardian of Anthony Wayne Butler at death of his father Edward Butler.

April   Journeyed to Washington in unsuccessful effort to win appointment as Governor of Louisiana Territory.

July 24   Resigned as judge because of financial obligations. Sold Hunter's Hill and moved to the Hermitage, continuing life of a planter and trader. Jackson later repurchased Hunter's Hill and owned it until financially pressed near the end of his life.

1805

May 11   Bought Truxton and became leader in Tennessee horse racing with stable at Clover Bottom, three miles from the Hermitage. Jackson's trading store was also moved to Clover Bottom.

May 29   Met Aaron Burr in Nashville, entertained him at the Hermitage, and supported Burr's Texas colonization prposals.

1806

May 30   Duel with Charles Dickinson arising out of strained relations and bets at a horse race. Jackson received a bullet close to his heart but killed Dickinson with a return shot.

September 24   Visited by Aaron Burr while Burr was en route to Kentucky to launch his Western expedition.

1807

January   Raised two brigades of militia in unsuccessful effort to capture Aaron Burr whose expedition floated down the Mississippi River.

June   Present at the trial of Burr in Richmond; believed Burr not guilty of treason.

1810

January   Adopted Andrew Jackson, Jr., infant son of Rachel's brother, Severn Donelson.

February   Applied for judgeship in Mississippi Territory, partly to escape attacks on his marriage to Rachel.

INDIAN WARS AND THE WAR OF 1812

1812

March 7   As Major General of Tennessee militia calls for volunteers in preparation for impending war with Great Britain.

June   Prepared for campaign against Creek Indians, believed to be allied with Tecumseh to check expansion of white settlement.

November   Commissioned Major General of United States volunteers; assembled a force of 2070 men in Nashville in December under his command.

1813

January 10   Set out by flatboat to support General Wilkinson at New Orleans.

February 6   Secretary of War Armstrong dismissed Jackson and his volunteers from service at Natchez in the expectation that the men would join Wilkinson's Regular Army forces and Jackson would be removed as a military rival.

March   Led his troops back to Tennessee, his personal strength on this march winning him the name, "Old Hickory."

September 4   Fight with the Benton brothers, Jesse and Thomas Hart, in Nashville. Jackson fell wounded in the arm and shoulder.

September 24   Though not fully recovered from his fight with the Bentons, Jackson organized a militia force to put down the Indian uprising among the Creeks following the massacre at Fort Mims in Mississippi Territory on August 30.

November 9   Defeated Creeks at Talladega, Alabama.

1814

January 21   Repulsed Indian attack at Emuckfaw Creek.

January 24   Withstood Indian attack at Enotachopco Creek.

March 27   Won decisive victory against the Creeks at the Horseshoe Bend of the Tallapoosa River, Alabama.

May 28   Appointed Major-General of Seventh Military District, including Tennessee, Louisiana and the Mississippi Territory.

August 9   Signed Treaty of Fort Jackson with Creek Indians, who surrendered twenty-three million acres in what is now Georgia and Alabama.

August 22   Pursued Creek and Seminole Indians into Florida, occupied Mobile and Fort Bowyer.

September 15   Held Fort Bowyer against British attack as British naval force prepared to move against New Orleans.

September 21   Issued Proclamation "To the Free Coloured Inhabitants of Louisiana" appealing for their services as soldiers of the United States.

November 7   Stormed Pensacola, defeated Spanish defenders as British moved out to sea.

December 1   Arrived in New Orleans to defend the city against British attack.

December 23   Opening of Battle of New Orleans with advance of the British under General Keane on the city.

1815

January 8   Victory over British troops under Major General Sir Edward Pakenham in final phase of the Battle of New Orleans, two weeks after treaty ending the War of 1812 had been signed.

March 31   Tried in the case of The United States v. Andrew Jackson for imprisoning Louis Louailler, a member of the Louisiana legislature in violation of a writ of **habeas corpus**. Jackson was found to be in contempt of court by Judge Hall and fined a thousand dollars and costs.

May 15   Returned to Nashville with Rachel and Andrew Jackson, Jr. Directed his aide, Major John Reid to begin a biography of Jackson.

November	Set out for Washington, met Thomas Jefferson at Lynchburg, Va., declared his support for James Monroe for President and ended speculation concerning his own candidacy.

1816

January	Death of John Reid, after which Jackson gave project of his biography to John H. Eaton of Franklin, Tenn., who published **The Life of Andrew Jackson** in 1817. A second edition was published in 1828.
March	Andrew J. Donelson left the Hermitage to enter West Point. His brother, John Donelson III, who had lived at the Hermitage died at this time.
September 14	Negotiated with Cherokee and later with Choctaw Indians for four million acres of land erroneously included in Treaty of Fort Jackson with the Creek Indians. Jackson agreed to payment of $180,000 to the Indians.

1817

April 22	Issued famous order directing that orders from the War Department to his subordinates must go through him. Led to conflict with General Winfield Scott and with President James Monroe who insisted on free exercise of his powers as Commander in Chief of the Army.
December 26	Secretary of War John Calhoun directed Jackson to lead an expedition against the Seminole Indians in Georgia. The Seminoles were charged with violating the Treaty of Jackson of 1814 and the Monroe administration sought also to acquire Florida.

1818

January	Church erected at the Hermitage by public subscription with Jackson one of the subscribers.
April 7	Took Spanish fort at St. Marks, Florida. Captured Alexander Arbuthnot, a Scottish Indian trader, and Robert C. Ambrister, a British marine. Jackson charged them with inciting and commanding the Indians, tried them by court-martial which found them guilty. They were put to death April 29.

May 24   Captured Pensacola from the Spanish, appointed a governor
and applied the revenue laws of the U.S.; ended First
Seminole War of 1817-1818.

May 30   Returned to Tennessee.

1819

January 3   Jackson arrived in Washington to defend his Florida
expedition.

February 8   Defeat by large majorities of resolutions backed by Henry
Clay in the House of Representatives censuring Jackson's
conduct in the Florida expedition. In President Monroe's
cabinet Jackson was defended by Secretary of State John
Quincy Adams and opposed by Secretary of the Treasury
William H. Crawford and Secretary of War John C.
Calhoun.

February 27   At Baltimore, while returning from journey to Philadelphia,
New York and West Point, learned of Adams-Onis Treaty
signed February 22 ceding Florida to the United States.

April   Returned to the "Second Hermitage" which had been
constructed in 1818.

1821

March 10   Commissioned as Governor of Florida.

June 1   Retired as commander of the Southern Division, U.S.
Army.

July 17   Took possession of Florida from Colonel José Callava
in Pensacola.

October 7   Left Florida with his family and returned to Tennessee.

PLANTER AND POLITICIAN

1822

June   Visited his plantation at Melton's Bluff on the Tennessee
River near Florence, Alabama, where he owned sixty
slaves.

July 20   Lower house of the Tennessee legislature nominated Jackson for President. The resolution was adopted in the senate on August 3.

1823

January 30   Commissioned Minister Plenipotentiary to Mexico to discuss the Annexation of Texas by the United States. Appointment was declined on February 19.

December 5   Took his seat in the U.S. Senate after election as Senator from Tennessee. Voted for many internal improvement bills and for tariff bills.

1824

January 8   Honored in Washington with a grand ball on anniversary of the Battle of New Orleans at which he was presented with the pistols given to Washington by Lafayette.

March 4   Nominated for the presidency by Pennsylvania state convention at Harrisburg.

April 26   Wrote letter in which he favored a "judicious tariff," supporting the Tariff of 1824 and Clay's American System, but opposed a national debt.

May   Departed from Washington for Tennessee, arriving in mid-June.

December 1   Won a plurality of 99 electoral votes for President over John Quincy Adams (84), William H. Crawford (41), and Henry Clay (37). Since this was not a majority the election went to the House of Representatives. John C. Calhoun elected Vice President.

December 7   Arrived in Washington with Rachel and Andrew J. Donelson.

1825

February 9   House of Representatives elected John Quincy Adams President with 13 votes to 7 for Jackson and 4 for William H. Crawford.

February 14   Referred to Clay as the "Judas of the West" who would "receive his thirty pieces of silver" in a letter to W. B.

Lewis, after being informed that Henry Clay had been offered the office of Secretary of State following his support for John Quincy Adams in the House presidential vote.

March   Returned to Tennessee traveling from Wheeling to Cincinnati on the steamboat **General Neville.**

October   Nominated again for President by the Tennessee legislature.

October 12   Resigned from the Senate.

1826

December   Martin Van Buren visited John C. Calhoun in Virginia and created coalition to support Jackson's election as President.

1827

January   **United States Telegraph**, newspaper organ of John C. Calhoun, edited by Duff Green in Washington, supported Jackson for President.

March   Albany **Argus**, Democratic newspaper in New York, came out for Jackson for President.

March   Martin Van Buren set out on a tour of the South to win support for Jackson in Virginia, North Carolina, South Carolina and Georgia.

April 27   Richmond **Enquirer** came out for Jackson for President.

1828

January 8   Attended reception in New Orleans on anniversary of his victory of 1814.

March 23   Cincinnati **Gazette** published attack on Jackson's marriage, followed soon after by similar attacks in the **National Journal** in Washington.

October 18   Coffin Handbill first printed by John Binns, editor of the Philadelphia **Democratic Press**.

October   Sold Melton's Bluff plantation in Alabama, which he had owned for more than a decade.

October	Death of Indian boy, Lincoyer, at the age of 16, raised by Jackson as one of his family since he had been orphaned at the Battle of Tallushatchee in 1813.
November 4	Elected President over John Quincy Adams by a popular vote of 647,286 to 508,064, followed by an electoral vote of 178 to 83. John C. Calhoun elected Vice President.
December 22	Death of Rachel Jackson caused, Jackson believed, by attacks on their marriage.
December 24	Rachel buried at the Hermitage.

THE FIRST TERM

1829

January 18	Left Tennessee for Washington traveling down the Cumberland to the Ohio and up the Ohio to Pittsburgh. Jackson was accompanied by Major W. B. Lewis, Andrew J. Donelson (who became his private secretary) and Emily Donelson.
February 12	Arrived in Washington.
March 4	Inaugurated as the seventh President of the United States.
August 25	Offered five million dollars for the purchase of Texas from Mexico, but the offer was refused.
September 10	Held Cabinet meeting in which he defended Margaret O'Neale Eaton, wife of Secretary of War John H. Eaton, against attacks on her by Washington society.
December 31	Wrote to John Overton giving his preference of Martin Van Buren over John C. Calhoun as his successor in the presidency.

1830

January 29	Jackson arranged a meeting between Secretary John H. Eaton and Secretary of the Navy John Branch to attempt a reconciliation in the Eaton affair.

February Summoned Cabinet Secretaries Ingham, Branch and Berrien and read paper directing that their wives accept Mrs. Eaton or that they leave the cabinet.

March 31 Nominated for President in Pennsylvania legislature. Nomination supported by other states.

April 13 Jackson gave toast at Jefferson Day dinner: "Our Union: it must be preserved." Calhoun replied: "The Union, next to our liberty, most dear."

May 27 Vetoed the Maysville Road bill.

May 28 Signed Indian Removal Act, providing for removal of Indians to lands west of the Mississippi River.

May 31 Vetoed bill authorizing subscription to stock of Washington Turnpike Company.

May 31 Signed bill for continuation of the Cumberland Road.

June 17 Set out with Andrew J. Donelson and Emily Donelson to make treaty at Franklin, Tennessee, for removal of the Choctaw and Chickasaw Indians. The Donelsons returned to Tennessee rather than call on Mrs. Eaton as Jackson requested.

August 27 Addressed delegation of the Chickasaw Indians about their consent to move west of the Mississippi River. Treaty was signed August 31. When this was not ratified by the Senate a second treaty was made October 20, 1832.

October 5 Negotiations with England culminated in Jackson's proclamation opening trade with the British West Indies which had been closed since the American Revolution.

December 7 First issue of the Washington **Globe,** newspaper edited by Francis B. Blair, established as the organ of the Jackson administration to replace Duff Green's **United States Telegraph,** which was under the influence of John C. Calhoun.

1831

February 22 Sent special message to Congress recommending the removal of the Cherokee Indians west of the Mississippi.

April 7   Resignation of Secretary of War John Eaton resolving the controversy over Margaret O'Neale Eaton in Jackson's official family. A general reorganization of the Cabinet followed in which all resigned except the Postmaster General, William T. Barry.

April 11   Resignation of Secretary of State Martin Van Buren.

April 19   Resignation of Secretary of the Treasury Samuel D. Ingham, which took effect June 20.

April 19   Resignation of Secretary of the Navy John Branch.

June 14   Wrote "Charleston letter" to citizens of that city in defense of the Union and attacking the doctrine of nullification. South Carolina appeared to have the support of Georgia in her defiance of the Supreme Court in the case of the Cherokee Indian, Corn Tassel.

June 15   Resignation of Attorney General John M. Berrien.

July 4   Concluded treaty with France (ratified February 2, 1832) in settlement of claims against France for spoliation against American commerce during the Napoleonic Wars. France agreed to payment of 25,000,000 francs payable in six annual installments.

July 26   John C. Calhoun wrote letter known as the Fort Hill Address publicly restating the ideas of his **Exposition and Protest** of 1828 and placing himself at the head of the nullification movement in South Carolina.

November 24 Andrew Jackson, Jr., married Sarah York in Philadelphia.

1832

January   Bullet removed from Jackson's left arm received in the fight with Jesse and Thomas Hart Benton in 1813. Thomas Hart Benton was now leading Jackson's attack against the Second Bank of the United States in the Senate.

January 25   Jackson's nomination of Martin Van Buren as minister to the Court of St. James defeated in the Senate by the deciding vote of Vice President John C. Calhoun.

February	Supported Georgia in its defiance of the Supreme Court in the case of Worcester **v.** Georgia involving the release of two missionaries imprisoned by Georgia while living among the Cherokees. Jackson was reported to have said, "John Marshall has made his decision, now let him enforce it."
April 6	Black Hawk War began after Sauk Indians under Black Hawk recrossed the Mississippi River into Illinois.
April 12	Drew up memorandum to guide Andrew Jackson, Jr., in the management of the Hermitage plantation. Extensive remodeling of the Hermitage begun in 1831 had been completed.
May 21-23	Nominated for a second term as President by the first national Democratic nominating convention. Martin Van Buren was nominated for Vice President. The two-thirds rule requiring a two-thirds majority for nomination was adopted at this convention.
July 10	Vetoed the bill to recharter the Second Bank of the United States in a message of 7000 words, the longest Presidential veto to this time.
July 14	Signed tariff bill which included limited reduction of duties.
August	Set out for the Hermitage accompanied by Francis Blair, returning to Washington October 19.
August 28	John C. Calhoun sent "Fort Hill letter" to Governor James Hamilton of South Carolina giving final statement of his theory of nullification and explaining his doctrine of the concurrent majority.
November 6	Jackson reelected to the Presidency over Henry Clay by a popular vote of 687,502 to 530,189 followed by an electoral vote of 219 to 49. Martin Van Buren elected Vice President.
November 24	South Carolina Ordinance of Nullification declared Tariff Acts of 1828 and 1832 null and void and prohibited their operation after February 1.

December 10   Issued the Nullification Proclamation to the people of South Carolina.

December 28   John C. Calhoun resigned as Vice President and took seat as Senator from South Carolina.

SECOND TERM
1833

March 2   Signed the Force Bill enacted in response to his request of January 16, 1833, for Congressional action to meet the nullification crisis in South Carolina.

March 2   Signed the Compromise Tariff Bill which had been introduced by Henry Clay in the House of Representatives.

March 18   South Carolina convention nullified the Force Act and repealed nullification of tariffs.

March 19   Submitted a list of five questions to the Cabinet on the relation of the government to the Second Bank of the United States.

March 20   Concluded treaty with Siam, first American treaty with a Far Eastern state.

May 6   Assaulted on board steamboat at Alexandria by Robert B. Randolph, a Navy lieutenant discharged with Jackson's approval.

June 6   Set out on journey to Philadelphia, New York and New England, riding on Baltimore and Ohio Railroad to Baltimore.

June 26   Awarded honorary degree of Doctor of Laws from Harvard University. Toured New England and suffered physical collapse at Concord, New Hampshire. Returned to Washington by steamboat, arriving July 4.

July 7   Death of General John Coffee, Jackson's general at New Orleans and close friend. Jackson wrote the inscription for his tombstone.

September 18 Read paper to his cabinet giving his arguments for removing the public deposits from the Second Bank of the United States on October 1.

September 23 Dismissed Secretary of the Treasury William J. Duane after he refused to order the removal of the public deposits from the Second Bank of the United States and appointed former Attorney General Roger B. Taney in his place.

September 26 Secretary of the Treasury Taney ordered removal of the deposits from the Second Bank of the United States to designated state banks. Removal began October 1.

November 14 Andrew Jackson Hutchings, Jackson's ward, married Mary Coffee.

December 4 Sent veto message to the Senate explaining his pocket veto of Henry Clay's bill to distribute surplus revenues from land sales to the states passed in the previous session of Congress.

December 26 Two resolutions introduced in the Senate by Henry Clay censuring executive proceedings in the removal of the public deposits from the Second Bank of the United States.

1834

January 29 Directed Secretary of War Lewis Cass to use Federal troops in labor riots on Chesapeake and Ohio Canal.

March 28 Senate resolution censoring Jackson for the removal of the public deposits from the Second Bank of the United States passed by vote of 26 to 20.

April As legal guardian of Andrew Jackson Hutchings since 1818, provided the latter with his estate when he reached his majority.

April 15 Jackson responded to the Senate censure resolution with a "Protest" which the Senate refused to enter on its journal.

April 24 Appointed John Eaton Governor in the Territory of Florida.

June 24	Senate rejected Jackson's appointment of Roger B. Taney as Secretary of the Treasury; the first Cabinet appointee to be rejected by that body.
August 5	Arrived at the Hermitage where he remained until October.
October 13	The Hermitage destroyed by fire. Rebuilding began immediately and was completed in 1835.

1835

January 8	Banquet in Washington celebrated the anniversary of the Battle of New Orleans at which Jackson celebrated also the extinguishment of the national debt.
January 30	Attempted assassination of Jackson in the rotunda of the Capitol by a deranged man, Richard Lawrence.
January	Appointment of Roger B. Taney as Associate Justice of the Supreme Court rejected by the Senate.
July 10	Left Washington for the newly rebuilt Hermitage, arriving August 4.
November 2	Second Seminole War begun by Osceola when Florida Seminoles refused to move west.

1836

January 18	Informed Congress of the refusal of the French to pay installments on the 25,000,000 franc settlement agreed to in the Treaty of 1832.
January 27	Great Britain offered mediation of spoilation claims controversy against France which was accepted by Jackson.
March 15	Appointment of Roger B. Taney to replace John Marshall as Chief Justice of the Supreme Court confirmed by the Senate.
June 23	Signed Deposit Act providing for public deposits in one bank in each state and for distribution of surplus funds in the Treasury to the states.
July	Authorized purchase of Texas, but not accepted by Mexico.

July 11	Issued Specie Circular (Treasury Order) requiring payment in specie for public lands in attempt to check speculation.
December 21	Sent special message to Congress deferring recognition of the independence of Texas from Mexico.

RETIREMENT

1837

January 16	Censure of Jackson in Senate is expunged by vote of 24 to 19 through efforts of Thomas Hart Benton.
March	Gave pocket veto to the bill to repeal the Specie Circular.
March 3	Recognized Texan independence and appointed a chargé d'affaires to the Republic of Texas.
March 4	Gave a Farewell Address to the American people.
March 6	Left Washington for the Hermitage.

1838

January-March	Suffered a winter of serious illness.

1839

July	Fulfilled promise to Rachel and joined the Presbyterian church in a service at the Hermitage.

1840

January 8	Attended the 25th anniversary of the Battle of New Orleans, partly to support the Democrats in the campaign of Martin Van Buren for the presidency, and partly to relieve the obligations of Andrew Jackson, Jr., incurred through Albert Ward in Memphis.

1842

December	Gave Amos Kendall permission and papers to write Jackson's biography, a portion of which was published in **Harper's Magazine**, but never completed.
February 24	Borrowed $10,000 from Francis Blair and John C. Rives in Washington, a debt not repaid before his death. The debt remained unpaid in 1855 and was finally met by a sale of lands from the Hermitage to the state of Tennessee.

1843

February 12   Wrote a letter to A. V. Brown, member of Congress from Tennessee, favoring immediate annexation of Texas which was used against the nomination of Martin Van Buren for President in the election of 1844.

June 7   Made new will.

1844

February 16   Congress remitted fine of $1000 ($2,732 with interest) levied against Jackson for contempt of court by Judge Hall in New Orleans in 1815.

October 22   Wrote widely published letter to General Robert Armstrong denying allegations by John Quincy Adams that Jackson had supported the exclusion of Texas in the Adams-Onis Treaty of 1819, ratified in 1821. Jackson supported James K. Polk over Henry Clay in the Election of 1844.

1845

June 8   Died at the Hermitage.

June 10   Burial at the Hermitage.

DOCUMENTS

FIRST INAUGURAL ADDRESS
March 4, 1829

Jackson's papers include two earlier drafts of his First Inaugural Address. They show that the major part of the address was composed by Jackson himself before he left the Hermitage and reveal few changes made later by his friends in Washington. Jackson spoke from the portico of the Capitol to a crowd so large and ill-mannered that some called it a triumph of the mob.

Fellow-Citizens: About to undertake the arduous duties that I have been appointed to perform by the choice of a free people, I avail myself of this customary and solemn occasion to express the gratitude which their confidence inspires and to acknowledge the accountability which my situation enjoins. . . .

In administering the laws of Congress I shall keep steadily in view the limitations as well as the extent of the Executive power, trusting thereby to discharge the functions of my office without transcending its authority. With foreign nations it will be my study to preserve peace and to cultivate friendship on fair and honorable terms, and in the adjustment of any differences that may exist or arise to exhibit the forbearance becoming a powerful nation rather than the sensibility belonging to a gallant people.

In such measures as I may be called on to pursue in regard to the rights of the separate States I hope to be animated by a proper respect for those sovereign members of our Union, taking care not to confound the powers they have reserved to themselves with those they have granted to the Confederacy.

The management of the public revenue—that searching operation in all governments—is among the most delicate and important trusts in ours, and it will, of course, demand no inconsiderable share of

21

my official solicitude. Under every aspect in which it can be considered it would appear that advantage must result from the observance of a strict and faithful economy. This I shall aim at the more anxiously both because it will facilitate the extinguishment of the national debt, the unnecessary duration of which is incompatible with real independence, and because it will counteract that tendency to public and private profligacy which a profuse expenditure of money by the Government is but too apt to engender. . . .

Internal improvement and the diffusion of knowledge, so far as they can be promoted by the constitutional acts of the Federal Government, are of high importance.

Considering standing armies as dangerous to free governments in time of peace, I shall not seek to enlarge our present establishment, nor disregard that salutary lesson of political experience which teaches that the military should be held subordinate to the civil power. . . . But the bulwark of our defense is the national militia, which in the present state of our intelligence and population must render us invincible. As long as our Government is administered for the good of the people, and is regulated by their will; as long as it secures to us the rights of person and of property, liberty of conscience and of the press, it will be worth defending; and so long as it is worth defending a patriotic militia will cover it with an impenetrable aegis. . . .

The recent demonstration of public sentiment inscribes on the list of Executive duties, in characters too legible to be overlooked, the task of reform, which will require particularly the correction of those abuses that have brought the patronage of the Federal Government into conflict with the freedom of elections, and the counteraction of those causes which have disturbed the rightful course of appointment and have placed or continued power in unfaithful or incompetent hands. . . .

A diffidence, perhaps too just, in my own qualifications will teach me to look with reverence to the examples of public virtue left by my illustrious predecessors, and with veneration to the lights that flow from the mind that founded and the mind that reformed our system. The same diffidence induces me to hope for instruction and aid from the coordinate branches of the Government, and for the indulgence and support of my fellow-citizens generally. And a firm reliance on the goodness of that Power whose providence mercifully protected our national infancy, and has since upheld our liberties in various vicissitudes, encourages me to offer up my ardent supplications that He will continue to make our beloved country the object of His divine care and gracious benediction.

FIRST ANNUAL MESSAGE
December 8, 1829

In his first annual message Jackson appealed for a constitutional revision of the method of selecting the President and Vice President through the electoral college or the House of Representatives, which he repeated unsuccessfully in each of his subsequent annual messages. This message also set forth Jackson's program to move the Indians west of the Mississippi River, which Congress supported in the Indian Removal Act of 1830.

Fellow-Citizens of the Senate and House of Representatives:
It affords me pleasure to tender my friendly greetings to you on the occasion of your assembling at the seat of Government to enter upon the important duties to which you have been called by the voice of our countrymen. The task devolves on me, under a provision of the Constitution, to present to you, as the Federal Legislature of twenty-four sovereign States and 12,000,000 happy people, a view of our affairs, and to propose such measures as in the discharge of my official functions have suggested themselves as necessary to promote the objects of our Union. . . .

Our foreign relations, although in their general character pacific and friendly, present subjects of difference between us and other powers of deep interest as well to the country at large as to many of our citizens. . . .

From France, our ancient ally, we have a right to expect that justice which becomes the sovereign of a powerful, intelligent, and magnanimous people. . . . The claims of our citizens for depredations upon their property, long since committed under the authority, and in many instances by the express direction, of the then existing Government of France, remain unsatisfied, and must therefore continue to furnish a subject of unpleasant discussion and possible collision between the two Governments. . . .

I consider it one of the most urgent of my duties to bring to your attention the propriety of amending that part of our Constitution which relates to the election of President and Vice-President. Our system of government was by its framers deemed an experiment, and they therefore consistently provided a mode of remedying its defects.

To the people belongs the right of electing their Chief Magistrate; it was never designed that their choice should in any case be defeated, either by the intervention of electoral colleges or by the agency confided, under certain contingencies, to the House of Representatives. . . .

The number of aspirants to the Presidency and the diversity of the interests which may influence their claims leave little reason to expect a choice in the first instance, and in that event the election must devolve on the House of Representatives, where it is obvious the will of the people may not be always ascertained, or, if ascertained, may not be regarded. . . . Honors and offices are at the disposal of the successful candidate. Repeated ballotings may make it apparent that a single individual holds the cast in his hand. May he not be tempted to name his reward? But even without corruption, supposing the probity of the Representative to be proof against the powerful motives by which it may be assailed, the will of the people is still constantly liable to be misrepresented. One may err from ignorance of the wishes of his constituents; another from a conviction that it is his duty to be governed by his own judgment of the fitness of the candidates; finally, although all were inflexibly honest, all accurately informed of the wishes of their constituents, yet under the present mode of election a minority may often elect a President, and when this happens it may reasonably be expected that efforts will be made on the part of the majority to rectify this injurious operation of their institutions. But although no evil of this character should result from such a perversion of the first principle of our system—that the majority is to govern—it must be very certain that a President elected by a minority can not enjoy the confidence necesssary to the successful discharge of his duties.

In this as in all other matters of public concern policy requires that as few impediments as possible should exist to the free operation of the public will. Let us, then, endeavor so to amend our system that the office of Chief Magistrate may not be conferred upon any citizen but in pursuance of a fair expression of the will of the majority.

I would therefore recommend such an amendment of the Constitution as may remove all intermediate agency in the election of the President and Vice-President. The mode may be so regulated as to preserve to each State its present relative weight in the election, and a failure in the first attempt may be provided for by confining the second to a choice between the two highest candidates. In connection with such an amendment it would seem advisable to limit the service of the Chief Magistrate to a single term of either four or six years. . .

There are, perhaps, few men who can for any great length of time enjoy office and power without being more or less under the influence of feelings unfavorable to the faithful discharge of their public duties.

Their integrity may be proof against improper considerations immediately addressed to themselves, but they are apt to acquire a habit of looking with indifference upon the public interests and of tolerating conduct from which an unpracticed man would revolt. Office is considered as a species of property, and government rather as a means of promoting individual interests than as an instrument created solely for the service of the people. Corruption in some and in others a perversion of correct feelings and principles divert government from its legitimate ends and make it an engine for the support of the few at the expense of the many. The duties of all public officers are, or at least admit of being made, so plain and simple that men of intelligence may readily qualify themselves for their performance; and I can not but believe that more is lost by the long continuance of men in office than is generally to be gained by their experience. I submit, therefore, to your consideration whether the efficiency of the Government would not be promoted and official industry and integrity better secured by a general extension of the law which limits appointments to four years. . . .

This state of the finances exhibits the resources of the nation in an aspect highly flattering to its industry and auspicious of the ability of Government in a very short time to extinguish the public debt. . . .

After the extinction of the public debt it is not probable that any adjustment of the tariff upon principles satisfactory to the people of the Union will until a remote period, if ever, leave the Government without a considerable surplus in the Treasury beyond what may be required for its current service. As, then, the period approaches when the application of the revenue to the payment of debt will cease, the disposition of the surplus will present a subject for the serious deliberation of Congress; and it may be fortunate for the country that it is yet to be decided. Considered in connection with the difficulties which have heretofore attended appropriations for purposes of internal improvement, and with those which this experience tells us will certainly arise whenever power over such subjects may be exercised by the General Government, it is hoped that it may lead to the adoption of some plan which will reconcile the diversified interests of the State and strengthen the bonds which unite them. Every member of the Union, in peace and in war, will be benefited by the improvement of inland navigation and the construction of highways in the several States. Let us, then, endeavor to attain this benefit in a mode which will be satisfactory to all. That hitherto adopted has by many of our fellow-citizens been deprecated as an infraction of the Constitution, while by others it has been viewed as inexpedient. . . .

To avoid these evils it appears to me that the most safe, just, and federal disposition which could be made of the surplus revenue would be its apportionment among the several States according to their ratio of representation, and should this measure not be found warranted by the Constitution that it would be expedient to propose to the States an amendment authorizing it. . . That this was intended to be a government of limited and specific, and not general, powers must be admitted by all, and it is our duty to preserve for it the character intended by its framers. If experience points out the necessity for an enlargement of these powers, let us apply for it to those for whose benefit it is to be exercised, and not undermine the whole system by a resort to overstrained constructions. The scheme has worked well. It has exceeded the hopes of those who devised it, and become an object of admiration to the world. We are responsible to our country and to the glorious cause of self-government for the preservation of so great a good. The great mass of legislation relating to our internal affairs was intended to be left where the Federal Convention found it—in the State governments. Nothing is clearer, in my view, than that we are chiefly indebted for the success of the Constitution under which we are now acting to the watchful and auxiliary operation of the State authorities. This is not the reflection of a day, but belongs to the most deeply rooted convictions of my mind. . . .

The condition and ulterior destiny of the Indian tribes within the limits of some of our States have become objects of much interest and importance. It has long been the policy of Government to introduce among them the arts of civilization, in the hope of gradually reclaiming them from a wandering life. This policy has, however. been coupled with another wholly incompatible with its success. Professing a desire to civilize and settle them, we have at the same time lost no opportunity to purchase their lands and thrust them farther into the wilderness. By this means they have not only been kept in a wandering state, but been led to look upon us an unjust and indifferent to their fate. Thus, though lavish in its expenditures upon the subject, Government has constantly defeated its own policy, and the Indians in general, receding farther and farther to the west, have retained their savage habits. A portion, however, of the Southern tribes, having mingled much with the whites and made some progress in the arts of civilized life, have lately attempted to erect an independent government within the limits of Georgia and Alabama. These States claiming to be the only sovereigns within their territories, extended their laws over the Indians, which induced the latter to call upon the United States for protection.

Under these circumstances the question presented was whether the General Government had a right to sustain those people in their pretensions. The Constitution declares that "no new State shall be formed or erected within the jurisdiction of any other State" without the consent of its legislature. If the General Government is not permitted to tolerate the erection of a confederate State within the territory of one of the members of this Union against her consent, much less could it allow a foreign and independent government to establish itself there. Georgia became a member of the Confederacy which eventuated in our Federal Union as a sovereign State, always asserting her claim to certain limits. . . . Alabama was admitted into the Union on the same footing with the original States, with boundaries which were prescribed by Congress. There is no constitutional, conventional, or legal provision which allows them less power over the Indians within their borders than is possessed by Maine or New York. . . .

Actuated by this view of the subject, I informed the Indians inhabiting parts of Georgia and Alabama that their attempt to establish an independent government would not be countenanced by the Executive of the United States, and advised them to emigrate beyond the Mississippi or submit to the laws of those States. . . .

A State can not be dismembered by Congress or restricted in the exercise of her constitutional power. But the people of those States and of every State, actuated by feelings of justice and a regard for our national honor, submit to you the interesting question whether something can not be done, consistently with the rights of the States, to preserve this much-injured race.

As a means of effecting this end I suggest for your consideration the propriety of setting apart an ample district west of the Mississippi, and without the limits of any State or Territory now formed, to be guaranteed to the Indian tribes as long as they shall occupy it, each tribe having a distinct control over the portion designated for its use. There they may be secured in the enjoyment of governments of their own choice, subject to no other control from the United States than such as may be necessary to preserve peace on the frontier and between the several tribes. There the benevolent may endeavor to teach them the arts of civilization, and, by promoting union and harmony among them, to raise up an interesting commonwealth, destined to perpetuate the race and to attest the humanity and justice of this Government.

This emigration should be voluntary, for it would be as cruel as unjust to compel the aborigines to abandon the graves of their fathers and seek a home in a distant land. But they should be distinctly informed that if they remain within the limits of the States they must be subject to their laws. In return for their obedience as individuals they will without doubt be protected in the enjoyment of those possessions which they have improved by their industry. . . .

The charter of the Bank of the United States expires in 1836, and its stockholders will most probably apply for a renewal of their privileges. In order to avoid the evils resulting from precipitancy in a measure involving such important principles and such deep pecuniary interests, I feel than I can not, in justice to the parties interested, too soon present it to the deliberate consideration of the Legislature and the people. Both the constitutionality and the expediency of the law creating this bank are well questioned by a large portion of our fellow-citizens, and it must be admitted by all that it has failed in the great end of establishing a uniform and sound currency.

Under these circumstances, if such an institution is deemed essential. to the fiscal operations of the Government, I submit to the wisdom of the Legislature whether a national one, founded upon the credit of the Government and its revenues, might not be devised which would avoid all constitutional difficulties and at the same time secure all the advantages to the Government and country that were expected to result from the present bank. . . .

ANDREW JACKSON

THE VETO OF THE MAYSVILLE ROAD BILL
May 27, 1830

*Jackson responded to the rising demands for national
aid to internal improvements with his veto of the
Maysville Road bill. His rejection was based more
on the local character of the road, which was confined to Kentucky, than on a narrow construction of
the Constitution. Moreover, Kentucky, was the home
of Henry Clay who opposed him politically and advo-
cated internal improvements along with a tariff in
his American System.*

To the House of Representatives.

Gentlemen: I have maturely considered the bill proposing to authorize "a subscription of stock in Maysville, Washington, Paris, and
Lexington Turnpike Road Company," and now return the same to
the House of Representatives, in which it originated, with my objections to its passage.

Sincerely friendly to the improvement of our country by means of
roads and canals, I regret that any difference of opinion in the mode
of contributing to it should exist between us. . . .

The constitutional power of the Federal Government to construct
or promote works of internal improvement presents itself in two points
of view —the first as bearing upon the sovereignty of the States within whose limits their execution is contemplated if jurisdiction of the
territory which they may occupy be claimed as necessary to their
preservation and use; the second as asserting the simple right to
appropriate money from the National Treasury in aid of such works
when undertaken by State authority, surrendering the claim of jurisdiction. In the first view the question of power is an open one,
and can be decided without the embarrassments attending the other,
arising from the practice of the Government. Although frequently and
strenuously attempted, the power to this extent has never been exercised by the Government in a single instance. It does not, in my
opinion, possess it; and no bill, therefore, which admits it can receive my official sanction.

But in the other view of the power the question is differently sit-
uated. The ground taken at an early period of the Government was
"that whenever money has been raised by the general authority and is
to be applied to a particular measure, a question arises whether the
particular measure be within the enumerated authorities vested in

Congress. If it be, the money requisite for it may be applied to it; if not, no such application can be made." The document in which this principle was first advanced is of deservedly high authority, and should be held in grateful remembrance for its immediate agency in rescuing the country from much existing abuse and for its conservative effect upon some of the most valuable principles of the Constitution. The symmetry and purity of the Government would doubtless have been better preserved if this restriction of the power of appropriation could have been maintained without weakening its ability to fulfill the general objects of its institution, an effect so likely to attend its admission, notwithstanding its apparent fitness, that every subsequent Administration of the Government, embracing a period of thirty out of the forty-two years of its existence, has adopted a more enlarged construction of the power. . . .

The bill before me does not call for a more definite opinion upon the particular circumstances which will warrant appropriations of money by Congress to aid works of internal improvement, for although the extension of the power to apply money beyond that of carrying into effect the object for which it is appropriated has, as we have seen, been long claimed and exercised by the Federal Government, yet such grants have always been professedly under the control of the general principle that the works which might be thus aided should be "of a general, not local, national, not State," character. A disregard of this distinction would of necessity lead to the subversion of the federal system. That even this is an unsafe one, arbitrary in its nature, and liable, consequently, to great abuses, is too obvious to require the confirmation of experience. It is, however, sufficiently definite and imperative to my mind to forbid my approbation of any bill having the character of the one under consideration. I have given to its provisions all the reflection demanded by a just regard for the interests of those of our fellow-citizens who have desired its passage, and by the respect which is due to a coordinate branch of the Government, but I am not able to view it in any other light than as a measure of purely local character, or if it can be considered national, that no further distinction between the appropriate duties of the General and State Governments need be attempted, for there can be no local interest that may not with equal propriety be denominated national. It has no connection with any established system of improvements; is exclusively within the limits of a State, starting at a point on the Ohio River and running out 60 miles to an interior town, and even as far as the State is interested conferring partial instead of general advantages. . . .

In the other view of the subject, and the only remaining one which it is my intention to present at this time, is involved the expediency of embarking in a system of internal improvement without a previous amendment of the Constitution explaining and defining the precise powers of the Federal Government over it. Assuming the right to appropriate money to aid in the construction of national works to be warranted by the cotemporaneous and continued exposition of the Constitution, its insufficiency for the successful prosecution of them must be admitted by all candid minds. If we look to usage to define the extent of the right, that will be found so variant and embracing so much that has been overruled as to involve the whole subject in great uncertainty and to render the execution of our respective duties in relation to it replete with difficulty and embarrassment. It is in regard to such works and the acquisition of additional territory that the practice obtained its first footing. In most, if not all other disputed questions of appropriation the construction of the Constitution may be regarded as unsettled if the right to apply money in the enumerated cases is placed on the ground of usage.

This subject has been one of much, and, I may add, painful, reflection to me. It has bearings that are well calculated to exert a powerful influence upon our hitherto prosperous system of government and which, on some accounts, may even excite despondency in the breast of an American citizen. I will not detain you with professions of zeal in the cause of internal improvements. If to be their friend is a virtue which deserves commendation, our country is blessed with an abundance of it, for I do not suppose there is an intelligent citizen who does not wish to see them flourish. But though all are their friends, but few, I trust, are unmindful of the means by which they should be promoted; none certainly are so degenerate as to desire their success at the cost of that sacred instrument with the preservation of which is indissolubly bound our country's hopes. . . .

If it be the wish of the people that the construction of roads and canals should be conducted by the Federal Government, it is not only highly expedient, but indispensably necessary, that a previous amendment of the Constitution, delegating the necessary power and defining and restricting its exercise with reference to the sovereignty of the States, should be made. Without it nothing extensively useful can be effected. The right to exercise as much jurisdiction as is necessary to preserve the works and to raise funds by the collection of tolls to keep them in repair can not be dispensed with. The Cumberland road should be an instructive admonition of the consequences of acting without this right. Year after year contests are witnessed, growing out of efforts to obtain the necessary appropriations for completing and repairing this useful work. Whilst one Congress may claim and exercise the power, a succeeding one may deny it; and this fluctuation of opinion must be unavoidably fatal to any scheme which from its extent would promote the interests and elevate the character of the country. The experience of the past has shown that the opinion of Congress is subject to such fluctuations. . . .

ANDREW JACKSON.

SECOND ANNUAL MESSAGE
December 6, 1830

In his Second Annual Message we find Jackson's defense of his Indian policy and his mounting concern for the issues of national aid to internal improvements, the tariff, and the Second Bank of the United States, the three most critical domestic conflicts in Jacksonian Democracy.

Fellow-Citizens of the Senate and House of Representatives:

The pleasure I have in congratulating you upon your return to your constitutional duties is much heightened by the satisfaction which the condition of our beloved country at this period justly inspires. . . .

The negotiation with France has been conducted by our minister with zeal and ability, and in all respects to my entire satisfaction. . . . The negotiation has been renewed with the present authorities, and, sensible of the general and lively confidence of our citizens in the justice and magnanimity of regenerated France, I regret the more not to have it in my power yet to announce the result so confidently anticipated. No ground, however, inconsistent with this expectation has yet been taken, and I do not allow myself to doubt that justice will soon be done us. The amount of the claims, the length of time they have remained unsatisfied, and their incontrovertible justice make an earnest prosecution of them by this Government an urgent duty. The illegality of the seizures and confiscations out of which they have arisen is not disputed, and whatever distinctions may have heretofore been set up in regard to the liability of the existing Government it is quite clear that such considerations can not now be interposed.. . .

Almost at the moment of the adjournment of your last session two bills—the one entitled"An act for making appropriations for building light-houses, light-boats, beacons, and monuments, placing buoys, and for improving harbors and directing surveys," and the other "An act to authorize a subscription for stock in the Louisville and Portland Canal Company"—were submitted for my approval. It was not possible within the time allowed me before the close of the session to give to these bills the consideration which was due to their character and importance, and I was compelled to retain them for that purpose. I now avail myself of this early opportunity to return them to the Houses in which they respectively originated with the reasons which, after mature deliberation, compel me to withhold my approval.

The practice of defraying out of the Treasury of the United States the expenses incurred by the establishment and support of light-houses, beacons, buoys, and public piers within the bays, inlets, harbors, and ports of the United States, to render the navigation thereof safe and easy, is coeval with the adoption of the Constitution, and has been continued without interruption or dispute. . . .

From a bill making direct appropriations for such objects I should not have withheld my assent. The one now returned does so in several particulars, but it also contains appropriations for surveys of a local character, which I can not approve. . . .

In speaking of direct appropriations I mean not to include a practice. . .of subscribing to the stock of private associations. . . .The practice of thus mingling the concerns of the Government with those of the States or of individuals is inconsistent with the object of its institution and highly impolitic. The successful operation of the federal system can only be preserved by confining it to the few and simple, but yet important, objects for which it was designed. . . .

The power which the General Government would acquire within the several States by becoming the principal stockholder in corporations, controlling every canal and each 60 or 100 miles of every important road, and giving a proportionate vote in all their elections, is almost inconceivable, and in my view dangerous to the liberties of the people. . .

In my objections to the bills authorizing subscritptions to the Maysville and Rockville road companies I expressed my views fully in regard to the power of Congress to construct roads and canals within a State or to appropriate money for improvements of a local character. I at the same time intimated my belief that the right to make appropriations for such as were of a national character had been so generally acted upon and so long acquiesced in by the Federal and State Governments and the constituents of each as to justify its exercise on the ground of continued and uninterrupted usage, but that it was, nevertheless, highly expedient that appropriations even of that character should, with the exception made at the time, be deferred until the national debt is paid, and that in the meanwhile some general rule for the action of the Government in that respect ought to be established.

These suggestions were not necessary to the decision of the question then before me, and were, I readily admit, intended to awake the attention and draw forth the opinions and observations of our constituents upon a subject of the highest importance to their interests, and one destined to exert a powerful influence upon the future operations of our political system. . . .

We have it constantly before our eyes that professions of superior zeal in the cause of internal improvement and a disposition to lavish the public funds upon objects of this character are daily and earnestly put forth by aspirants to power as constituting the highest claims to the confidence of the people. Would it be strange, under such circumstances, and in times of great excitement, that grants of this description should find their motives in objects which may not accord with the public good? Those who have not had occasion to see and regret the indication of a sinister influence in these matters in past times have been more fortunate than myself in their observation of the course of public affairs. . .

Thus viewing the subject, I have heretofore felt it my duty to recommend the adoption of some plan for the distribution of the surplus funds, which may at any time remain in the Treasury after the national debt shall have been paid, among the States, in proportion to the number of their Representatives, to be applied by them to objects of internal improvement. . . .

In my first message I stated it to be my opinion that "it is not probable that any adjustment of the tariff upon principles satisfactory to the people of the Union will until a remote period, if ever, leave the Government without a considerable surplus in the Treasury beyond what may be required for its current service." I have had no cause to change that opinion, but much to confirm it. Should these expectations be realized, a suitable fund would thus be produced for the plan under consideration to operate upon, and if there be no such fund its adoption will, in my opinion, work no injury to any interest. . .

It may sometime happen that the interests of particular States would not be deemed to coincide with the general interest in relation to improvements within such States. But if the danger to be apprehended from this source is sufficient to require it, a discretion might be reserved to Congress to direct to such improvement of a general character as the States concerned might not be disposed to unite in, the application of the quotas of those States, under the restriction of confining to each State the expenditure of its appropriate quota. It may, however, be assumed as a safe general rule that such improvements as serve to increase the prosperity of the respective States in which they are made, by giving new facilities to trade, and thereby augmenting the wealth and comfort of their inhabitants, constitute the surest mode of conferring permanent and substantial advantages upon the whole. The strength as well as the true glory of the Confederacy is founded on the prosperity and power of the several independent sovereignties of which it is composed and the certainty with which they can be brought into successful active cooperation through the agency of the Federal Government. . . .

After all, the nature of the subject does not admit of a plan wholly free from objection. That which has for some time been in operation is, perhaps, the worst that could exist, and every advance that can be made in its improvement is a matter eminently worthy of your most deliberate attention. . . .

Any mode which is calculated to give the greatest degree of effect and harmony to our legislation upon the subject, which shall best serve to keep the movement of the Federal Government within the sphere intended by those who modeled and those who adopted it, which shall lead to the extinguishment of the national debt in the shortest period and impose the lightest burthens upon our constituents, shall receive from me a cordial and firm support. . . .

It gives me pleasure to announce to Congress that the benevolent policy of the Government, steadily pursued for nearly thirty years, in relation to the removal of the Indians beyond the white settlements is approaching to a happy consummation. Two important tribes have accepted the provisions made for their removal at the last session of Congress, and it is believed that their example will induce the remaining tribes also to seek the same obvious advantages.

The consequences of a speedy removal will be important to the United States, to individual States, and to the Indians themselves. The pecuniary advantages which it promises to the Government are the least of its recommendations. It puts an end to all possible danger of collision between the authorities of the General and State Government on account of the Indians. It will place a dense and civilized population in large tracts of country now occupied by a few savage hunters. By opening the whole territory between Tennessee on the north and Louisiana on the south to the settlement of the whites it will incalculably strengthen the southwestern frontier and render the adjacent States strong enough to repel future invasions without remote aid. It will relieve the whole State of Mississippi and the western part of Alabama of Indian occupancy and enable those States to advance rapidly in population, wealth, and power. It will separate the Indians from immediate contact with settlements of whites; free them from the power of the States; enable them to pursue happiness in their own way and under their own rude institutions; will retard the progress of decay, which is lessening their numbers, and perhaps cause them gradually, under the protection of the Government and through the influence of good counsels, to cast off their savage habits and become an interesting, civilized, and Christian community. These consequences, some of them so certain and the rest so probable, make the complete execution of the plan sanctioned by Congress at their last session an object of much solicitude. . . .

With a full understanding of the subject, the Choctaw and the Chickasaw tribes have with great unanimity determined to avail themselves of the liberal offers presented by the act of Congress, and have agreed to remove beyond the Mississippi River. . . .

Humanity has often wept over the fate of the aborigines of this country, and Philanthropy has been long busily employed in devising means to avert it, but its progress has never for a moment been arrested, and one by one have many powerful tribes disappeared from the earth. To follow to the tomb the last of his race and to tread on the graves of extinct nations excite melancholy reflections. But true philanthropy reconciles the mind to these vicissitudes as it does to the extinction of one generation to make room for another. . . .

Philanthropy could not wish to see this continent restored to the condition in which it was found by our forefathers. What good man would prefer a country covered with forests and ranged by a few thousand savages to our extensive Republic, studded with cities, towns, and prosperous farms, embellished with all the improvements which art can devise or industry execute, occupied by more than 12,000,000 happy people, and filled with all the blessings of liberty, civilization, and religion?. . .

The waves of population and civilization are rolling to the westward, and we now propose to acquire the countries occupied by the red men of the South and West by a fair exchange, and, at the expense of the United States, to send them to a land where their existence may be prolonged and perhaps made perpetual. Doubtless it will be painful to leave the graves of their fathers; but what do they more than our ancestors did or than our children are now doing? To better their condition in an unknown land our forefathers left all that was dear in earthly objects. Our children by thousands yearly leave the land of their birth to seek new homes in distant regions. Does Humanity weep at these painful separations from everything, animate and inanimate, with which the young heart has become entwined? Far from it. It is rather a source of joy that our country affords scope where our young population may range unconstrained in body or in mind, developing the power and faculties of man in their highest perfection. . . .

And is it supposed that the wandering savage has a stronger attachment to his home than the settled, civilized Christian? Is it more afflicting to him to leave the graves of his fathers than it is to our brothers and children? Rightly considered, the policy of the General Government toward the red man is not only liberal but generous. He is unwilling to submit to the laws of the States and mingle with their population. To save him from this alternative, or perhaps utter annihilation, the General Government kindly offers him a new home, and proposes to pay the whole expense of his removal and settlement. . . .

It is, therefore, a duty which this Government owes to the new States to extinguish as soon as possible the Indian title to all lands which Congress themselves have included within their limits. . . .

The difficulties of a more expedient adjustment of the present tariff, although great, are far from being insurmountable. Some are unwilling to improve any of its parts because they would destroy the whole; others fear to touch the objectionable parts lest those they approve should be jeoparded. I am persuaded that the advocates of these conflicting views do injustice to the American people and to their representatives. The general interest is the interest of each, and my confidence is entire that to insure the adoption of such modifications of the tariff as the general interest requires it is only necessary that that interest should be understood.

It is an infirmity of our nature to mingle our interests and prejudices with the operation of our reasoning powers, and attribute to the objects of our likes and dislikes qualities they do not possess and effects they can not produce. The effects of the present tariff are doubtless overrated, both in its evils and in its advantages. By one class of reasoners the reduced price of cotton and other agricultural products is ascribed wholly to its influence, and by another the reduced price of manufactured articles. The probability is that neither opinion approaches the truth, and that both are induced by that influence of interests and prejudices to which I have referred. The decrease of prices extends throughout the commercial world, embracing not only the raw material and the manufactured article, but provisions and lands. The cause must therefore be deeper and more pervading than the tariff of the United States. . . .

While the chief object of duties should be revenue, they may be so adjusted as to encourage manufacturers. In this adjustment, however, it is the duty of the Government to be guided by the general good. Objects of national importance alone ought to be protected. Of these the productions of our soil, our mines, and our workshops, essential to national defense, occupy the first rank. Whatever other species of domestic industry, having the importance to which I have referred, may be expected, after temporary protection, to compete with foreign labor on equal terms merit the same attention in a subordinate degree.

The present tariff taxes some of the comforts of life unnecessarily high; it undertakes to protect interests too local and minute to justify a general exaction, and it also attempts to force some kinds of manufacturers for which the country is not ripe. Much relief will be derived in some of these respects from the measures of your last session. . . .

That our deliberations on this interesting subject should be uninfluenced by those partisan conflicts that are incident to free institutions is the fervent wish of my heart. To make this great question, which unhappily so much divides and excites the public mind, subservient to the short-sighted views of faction must destroy all hope of settling it satisfactorily to the great body of the people and for the general interest. I can not, therefore, in taking leave of the subject, too earnestly for my own feeling or the common good warn you against the blighting consequences of such a course. . . .

The importance of the principles involved in the inquiry whether it will be proper to recharter the Bank of the United States requires that I should again call the attention of Congress to the subject. Nothing has occurred to lessen in any degree the dangers which many of our citizens apprehend from that institution as at present organized. In the spirit of improvement and compromise which distinguishes our country and its institutions it becomes us to inquire whether it be not possible to secure the advantages afforded by the present bank through the agency of a Bank of the United States so modified in its principles and structure as to obviate constitutional and other objections.

It is thought practicable to organize such a bank with the necessary officers as a branch of the Treasury Department, based on the public and individual deposits, without power to make loans or purchase property, which shall remit the funds of the Government, and the expense of which may be paid, if thought advisable, by allowing its officers to sell bills of exchange to private individuals at a moderate premium. Not being a corporate body, having no stockholders, debtors, or property, and but few officers, it would not be obnoxious to the constitutional objections which are urged against the present bank; and having no means to operate on the hopes, fears, or interests of large masses of the community, it would be shorn of the influence which makes that bank formidable. The States would be strengthened by having in their hands the means of furnishing the local paper currency through their own banks, while the Bank of the United States, though issuing no paper, would check the issues of the State banks by taking their notes in deposit and for exchange only

so long as they continue to be redeemed with specie. In times of public emergency the capacities of such an institution might be enlarged
by legislative provisions.

These suggestions are made not so much as a recommendation as
with a view of calling the attention of Congress to the possible modifications of a system which can not continue to exist in its present
form without occasional collisions with the local authorities and perpetual apprehensions and discontent on the part of the States and the
people. . . .

ANDREW JACKSON

THIRD ANNUAL MESSAGE
December 6, 1831

Shortest of all Jackson's annual messages, the third announced the treaty to settle our claims against France growing out of spoliations committed during the Napoleonic Wars, anticipated the extinguishment of the public debt, and closed with an allusion to the coming crisis over the tariff.

In my message at the opening the last session of Congress I expressed a confident hope that the justice of our claims upon France, urged as they were with perseverance and signal ability by our minister there, would finally be acknowledged. This hope has been realized. A treaty has been signed which will immediately be laid before the Senate for its approbation, and which, containing stipulations that require legislative acts, must have the concurrence of both Houses before it can be carried into effect. By it the French Government engage to pay a sum which, if not quite equal to that which may be found due to our citizens, will yet, it is believed, under all circumstances, be deemed satisfactory by those interested. . . . A comparatively small sum is stipulated on our part to go to the extinction of all claims by French citizens on our Government, and a reduction of duties on our cotton and their wines has been agreed on as a consideration for the renunciation of an important claim for commercial privileges under the construction they gave to the treaty for the cession of Louisiana.

Should this treaty receive the proper sanction, a source of irritation will be stopped that has for so many years in some degree alienated from each other two nations who, from interest as well as the remembrance of early associations, ought to cherish the most friendly relations; an encouragement will be given for perseverance in the demands of justice by this new proof that if steadily pursued they will be listened to, and admonition will be offered to those powers, if any, which may be inclined to evade them that they will never be abandoned; above all, a just confidence will be inspired in our fellow-citizens that their Government will exert all the powers with which they have invested it in support of their just claims upon foreign nations; at the same time that the frank acknowledgment and provision for the payment of those which were addressed to our equity, although unsupported by legal proof, affords a practical illustration of our submission to the divine rule of doing to others what we desire they should do unto us. . . .

The internal peace and security of our confederated States is the next principal object of the General Government. Time and experience have proved that the abode of the native Indian within their limits is dangerous to their peace and injurious to himself. In accordance with my recommendation at a former session of Congress, an appropriation of half a million of dollars was made to aid the voluntary removal of the various tribes beyond the limits of the States. At the last session I had the happiness to announce that the Chickasaws and Choctaws had accepted the generous offer of the Government and agreed to remove beyond the Mississippi River, by which the whole of the State of Mississippi and the western part of Alabama will be freed from Indian occupancy and opened to a civilized population. . . .

At the request of the authorities of Georgia the registration of Cherokee Indians for emigration has been resumed, and it is confidently expected that one-half, if not two-thirds, of that tribe will follow the wise example of their more westerly brethren. . . .

During the present year the attention of the Government has been particularly directed to those tribes in the powerful and growing State of Ohio, where considerable tracts of the finest lands were still occupied by the aboriginal proprietors. Treaties, either absolute or conditional, have been made extinguishing the whole Indian title to the reservations in that State, and the time is not distant, it is hoped, when Ohio will be no longer embarrassed with the Indian population. The same measures will be extended to Indiana as soon as there is reason to anticipate success. It is confidently believed that perseverance for a few years in the present policy of the Government will extinguish the Indian title to all lands lying within the States composing our Federal Union, and remove beyond their limits every Indian who is not willing to submit to their laws. Thus will all conflicting claims to jurisdiction between the States and the Indian tribes be put to rest. It is pleasing to reflect that results so beneficial, not only to the States immediately concerned, but to the harmony of the Union, will have been accomplished by measures equally advantageous to the Indians. What the native savages become when surrounded by a dense population and by mixing with the whites may be seen in the miserable remnants of a few Eastern tribes, deprived of political and civil rights, forbidden to make contracts, and subjected to guardians, dragging out a wretched existence, without excitement, without hope, and almost without thought. . . .

From the large importations of the present years it may be safely estimated that the revenue which will be received into the Treasury from that source during the next year, with the aid of that received from the public lands, will considerably exceed the amount of the receipts of the present year; and it is believed that with the means which the Government will have at its disposal from various sources, which will be fully stated by the proper Department, the whole of the public debt may be extinguished, either by redemption or purchase, within the four years of my Administration. We shall then exhibit the rare example of a great nation, abounding in all the means of happiness and security, altogether free from debt.

The confidence with which the extinguishment of the public debt may be anticipated presents an opportunity for carrying into effect more fully the policy in relation to import duties which has been recommended in my former messages. A modification of the tariff which shall produce a reduction of our revenue to the wants of the Government and an adjustment of the duties on imports with a view to equal justice in relation to all our national interests and to the counteraction of foreign policy so far as it may be injurious to those interests, is deemed to be one of the principal objects which demand the consideration of the present Congress. Justice to the interests of the merchant as well as the manufacturer requires that material reductions in the import duties be prospective; and unless the present Congress shall dispose of the subject the proposed reductions can not properly be made to take effect at the period when the necessity for the revenue arising from present rates shall cease. It is therefore desirable that arrangements be adopted at your present session to relieve the people from unnecessary taxation after the extinguishment of the public debt. In the exercise of that spirit of concession and conciliation which has distinguished the friends of our Union in all great emergencies, it is believed that this object may be effected without injury to any national interest. . . .

The extension of the judiciary system of the United States is deemed to be one of the duties of Government. One-fourth of the States in the Union do not participate in the benefits of a circuit court. To the States of Indiana, Illinois, Missouri, Alabama, Mississippi, and Louisiana, admitted into the Union since the present judicial system was organized, only a district court has been allowed. If this be sufficient, then the circuit courts already existing in eighteen States ought to be abolished; if it be not sufficient, the defect ought to be remedied, and these States placed on the same footing with the other members of the Union. . . .

Entertaining the opinions heretofore expressed in relation to the Bank of the United States as at present organized, I felt it my duty in my former messages frankly to disclose them, in order that the

attention of the Legislature and the people should be seasonably directed to that important subject, and that it might be considered and
finally disposed of in a manner best calculated to promote the ends
of the Constitution and subserve the public interests. Having thus
conscientiously discharged a constitutional duty, I deem it proper on
this occasion, without a more particular reference to the views of the
subject then expressed, to leave it for the present to the investigation
of an enlightened people and their representatives.

In conclusion permit me to invoke that Power which superintends
all governments to infuse into your deliberations at this important
crisis of our history a spirit of mutual forbearance and conciliation. In
that spirit was our Union formed, and in that spirit must it be preserved.

ANDREW JACKSON.

THE VETO OF THE BANK BILL
July 10, 1832

Nicholas Biddle, President of the Second Bank of the United States, joined with Henry Clay and others to introduce a bill in Congress to recharter the bank in 1832, four years before the charter expired. They hoped to gain advantage from the politics of a presidential election year. The bill passed House and Senate but was promptly rejected by Jackson in a message written with the assistance of Amos Kendall, Roger B. Taney, Andrew J. Donelson and Levi Woodbury. The document is crucial to Jacksonian Democracy and has been called by one authority "the most important presidential veto in American history." In it, Jackson challenged the opinion of the Supreme Court in the case of McCulloch v. Maryland.

To the Senate:

The bill "to modify and continue" the act entitled "An act to incorporate the subscribers to the Bank of the United States" was presented to me on the 4th July instant. Having considered it with that solemn regard to the principles of the Constitution which the day was calculated to inspire, and come to the conclusion that it ought not to become a law, I herewith return it to the Senate, in which it originated, with my objections.

A bank of the United States is in many respects convenient for the Government and useful to the people. Entertaining this opinion, and deeply impressed with the belief that some of the powers and privileges possessed by the existing bank are unauthorized by the Constitution, subversive of the rights of the States, and dangerous to the liberties of the people, I felt it my duty at an early period of my Administration to call the attention of Congress to the practicability of organizing an institution combining all its advantages and obviating these objections. I sincerely regret that in the act before me I can perceive none of those modifications of the bank charter which are necessary, in my opinion, to make it compatible with justice, with sound policy, or with the Constitution of our country.

The present corporate body, denominated the president, directors, and company of the Bank of the United States, will have existed at the time this act is intended to take effect twenty years. It enjoys an exclusive privilege of banking under the authority of the General Government, a monopoly of its favor and support, and, as a necessary consequence, almost a monopoly of the foreign and domestic exchange. The powers, privileges, and favors bestowed upon it in the original charter, by increasing the value of the stock far above its par value, operated as a gratuity of many millions to the stockholders. . . .

The act before me proposes another gratuity to the holders of the same stock, and in many cases to the same men, of at least seven millions more. . . . On all hands it is conceded that its passage will increase at least 20 or 30 per cent more the market price of the stock, subject to the payment of the annuity of $200,000 per year secured by the act, thus adding in a moment one-fourth to its par value. It is not our own citizens only who are to receive the bounty of our Government. More than eight millions of the stock of this bank are held by foreigners. By this act the American Republic proposes virtually to make them a present of some millions of dollars. For these gratuities to foreigners and to some of our own opulent citizens the act secures no equivalent whatever. . . .

Every monopoly and all exclusive privileges are granted at the expense of the public, which ought to receive a fair equivalent. The many millions which this act proposes to bestow on the stockholders of the existing bank must come directly or indirectly out of the earnings of the American people. It is due to them, therefore, if their Government sell monopolies and exclusive privileges, that they should at least exact for them as much as they are worth in open market. The value of the monopoly in this case may be correctly ascertained. The twenty-eight millions of stock would probably be at an advance of 50 per cent, and command in market at least $42,000,000, subject to the payment of the present bonus. The present value of the monopoly, therefore, is $17,000,000, and this the act proposes to sell for three millions, payable in fifteen annual installments of $200,000 each.

It is not conceivable how the present stockholders can have any claim to the special favor of the Government. The present corporation has enjoyed its monopoly during the period stipulated in the original contract. If we must have such a corporation, why should not the Government sell out the whole stock and thus secure to the people the full market value of the privileges granted? Why should not Congress create and sell twenty-eight millions of stock, incorporating the purchasers with all the powers and privileges secured in this act and putting the premium upon the sales into the Treasury?

But this act does not permit competition in the purchase of this monopoly. It seems to be predicated on the erroneous idea that the present stockholders have a prescriptive right not only to the favor but to the bounty of Government. It appears that more than a fourth part of the stock is held by foreigners and the residue is held by a few hundred of our own citizens, chiefly of the richest class. . . .

If our Government must sell monopolies, it would seem to be its duty to take nothing less than their full value, and if gratuities must be made once in fifteen or twenty years let them not be bestowed on the subjects of a foreign government nor upon a designated and favored class of men in our own country. It is but justice and good policy, as far as the nature of the case will admit, to confine our favors to our own fellow citizens, and let each in his turn enjoy an opportunity to profit by our bounty. In the bearings of the act before me upon these points I find ample reasons why it should not become a law....

The modifications of the existing charter proposed by this act are not such, in my view, as make it consistent with the rights of the States or the liberties of the people. The qualification of the right of the bank to hold real estate, the limitation of its power to establish branches, and the power reserved to Congress to forbid the circulation of small notes are restrictions comparatively of little value or importance. All the objectionable principles of the existing corporation, and most of its odious features, are retained without alleviation. . . .

Is there no danger to our liberty and independence in a bank that in its nature has so little to bind it to our country? The president of the bank has told us that most of the State banks exist by its forbearance. Should its influence become concentered, as it may under the operation of such an act as this, in the hands of a self-elected directory whose interests are identified with those of the foreign stockholders, will there not be cause to tremble for the purity of our elections in peace and for the independence of our country in war? Their power would be great whenever they might choose to exert it; but if this monopoly were regularly renewed every fifteen or twenty years on terms proposed by themselves, they might seldom in peace put forth their strength to influence elections or control the affairs of the nation. But if any private citizen or public functionary should interpose to curtail its powers or prevent a renewal of its privileges, it can not be doubted that he would be made to feel its influence.

Should the stock of the bank principally pass into the hands of the subjects of a foreign country, and we should unfortunately become involved in a war with that country, what would be our condition? Of the course which would be pursued by a bank almost wholly owned by the subjects of a foreign power, and managed by those whose interests, if not affections, would run in the same direction there can be no doubt. All its operations within would be in aid of the hostile fleets and armies without. Controlling our currency, receiving our public moneys, and holding thousands of our citizens in dependence, it would be more formidable and dangerous than the naval and military power of the enemy.

If we must have a bank with private stockholders, every consideration of sound policy and every impulse of American feeling admonishes that it should be purely American. Its stockholders should be composed exclusively of our own citizens, who at least ought to be friendly to our Government and willing to support it in times of difficulty and danger. . . .

It is maintained by the advocates of the bank that its constitutionality in all its features ought to be considered as settled by precedent and by the decision of the Supreme Court. To this conclusion I can not assent. Mere precedent is a dangerous source of authority, and should not be regarded as deciding questions of constitutional power except where the acquiescence of the people and the States can be considered as well settled. So far from this being the case on this subject, an argument against the bank might be based on precedent. One Congress, in 1791, decided in favor of a bank; another, in 1811, decided against it. One Congress in 1815, decided against a bank; another, in 1816, decided in its favor. Prior to the present Congress, therefore, the precedents drawn from that source were equal. If we resort to the States, the expressions of legislative, judicial, and executive opinions against the bank have been probably to those in its favor as 4 to 1. There is nothing in precedent, therefore, which, if its authority were admitted, ought to weigh in favor of the act before me.

If the opinion of the Supreme Court covered the whole ground of this act, it ought not to control the coordinate authorities of this Government. The Congress, the Executive and the Court must each for itself be guided by its own opinion of the Constitution. Each public officer who takes an oath to support the Constitution swears that he will support it as he understands it, and not as it is understood by others. It is as much the duty of the House of Representatives, of the Senate, and of the President to decide upon the constitutionality of any bill or resolution which may be presented to them for passage or approval as it is of the supreme judges when it may be brought before them for judicial decision. The opinion of the judges has no more authority over Congress than the opinion of Congress has over the judges, and on that point the President is independent of both. The authority of the Supreme Court must not, therefore, be permitted to control the Congress or the Executive when acting in their legislative capacities, but to have only such influence as the force of their reasoning may deserve.

But in the case relied upon the Supreme Court have not decided that all the features of this corporation are compatible with the Constitution. It is true that the court have said that the law incorporating the bank is a constitutional exercise of power by Congress; but taking into view the whole opinion of the court and the reasoning by which they have come to that conclusion, I understand them to have decided that inasmuch as a bank is an appropriate means for carrying into effect the enumerated powers of the General Government, therefore the law incorporating it is in accordance with that provision of the Constitution which declares that Congress shall have power "to make all laws which shall be necessary and proper for carrying those powers into execution." Having satisfied themselves that the word "necessary" in the Constitution means "needful," "requisite," "essential," "conductive to," and that "a bank" is a convenient, a useful, and essential instrument in the prosecution of the Government's "fiscal operations," they conclude that to "use one must be within the discretion of Congress" and that "the act to incorporate the Bank of the United States is a law made in pursuance of the Constitution"; "but," say they, "where the law is not prohibited and is really calculated to effect any of the objects intrusted to the Government, to undertake here to inquire into the degree of its necessity would be to pass the line which circumscribes the judicial department and to tread on legislative ground."

The principle here affirmed is that the "degree of its necessity," involving all the details of a banking institution, is a question exclusively for legislative consideration. A bank is constitutional, but it is the province of the Legislature to determine whether this or that particular power, privilege, or exemption is "necessary and proper" to enable the bank to discharge its duties to the Government, and from their decision there is no appeal to the courts of justice. Under the decision of the Supreme Court, therefore, it is the exclusive province of Congress and the President to decide whether the particular features of this act are necessary and proper in order to enable the bank to perform conveniently and efficiently the public duties assigned to it as a fiscal agent, and therefore constitutional, or unnecessary and improper, and therefore unconstitutional.

Without commenting on the general principle affirmed by the Supreme Court, let us examine the details of this act in accordance with the rule of legislative action which they have laid down. It will be found that many of the powers and privileges conferred on it can not be supposed necessary for the purpose for which it is proposed to be created, and are not, therefore, means necessary to attain the end in view, and consequently not justified by the Constitution. . . .

reasons — In another point of view this provision is a palpable attempt to
uhConsl. amend the Constitution by an act of legislation. The Constitution declares that "the Congress shall have power to exercise exclusive legislation in all cases whatsoever" over the District of Columbia. Its constitutional power, therefore, to establish banks in the District of Columbia and increase their capital at will is unlimited and uncontrollable by any other power than that which gave authority to the Constitution. Yet this act declares that Congress shall not increase the capital of existing banks, nor create other banks with capitals exceeding in the whole $6,000,000. The Constitution declares that Congress shall have power to exercise exclusive legislation over this District "in all cases whatsoever," and this act declares they shall not. Which is the supreme law of the land? This provision can not be "necessary" or "proper" or constitutional unless the absurdity be admitted that whenever it be "necessary and proper" in the opinion of Congress they have a right to barter away one portion of the powers vested in them by the Constitution as a means of executing the rest. . . .

— The Government is the only "proper" judge where its agents should reside and keep their offices, because it best knows where their presence will be "necessary." It can not, therefore, be "necessary" or "proper" to authorize the bank to locate branches where it pleases to perform the public service, without consulting the Government, and contrary to its will. The principle laid down by the Supreme Court concedes that Congress can not establish a bank for purposes of private speculation and gain, but only as a means of executing the delegated powers of the General Government. By the same principle a branch bank can not constitutionally be established for other than public purposes. The power which this act gives to establish two branches in any State, without the injunction or request of the Government and for other than public purposes, is not "necessary" to the due execution of the powers delegated to Congress. . . .

The principle is conceded that the States can not rightfully tax the operations of the General Government. They can not tax the money of the Government deposited in the State banks, nor the agency of those banks in remitting it; but will any man maintain that their mere selection to perform this public service for the General Government would exempt the State banks and their ordinary business from State taxation? Had the United States, instead of establishing a bank at Philadelphia, employed a private banker to keep and transmit their funds, would it have deprived Pennsylvania of the right to tax his bank and his usual banking operations? It will not be pretended. . . .

It can not be necessary to the character of the bank as a fiscal agent of the Government that its private business should be exempted from that taxation to which all the State banks are liable, nor can I conceive it "proper" that the substantive and most essential powers reserved by the States shall be thus attacked and annihilated as a means of executing the powers delegated to the General Government. It may be safely assumed that none of those sages who had an agency in forming or adopting our Constitution ever imagined that any portion of the taxing power of the States not prohibited to them nor delegated to Congress was to be swept away and annihilated as a means of executing certain powers delegated to Congress.

If our power over means is so absolute that the Supreme Court will not call in question the constitutionality of an act of Congress the subject of which "is not prohibited, and is really calculated to effect any of the objects intrusted to the Government," although, as in the case before me, it takes away powers expressly granted to Congress and rights scrupulously reserved to the States, it becomes us to proceed in our legislation with the utmost caution. Though not directly, our own powers and the rights of the States may be indirectly legislated away in the use of means to execute substantive powers. We may not enact that Congress shall not have the power of exclusive legislation over the District of Columbia, but we may pledge the faith of the United States that as a means of executing other powers it shall not be exercised for twenty years or forever. We may not pass an act prohibiting the States to tax the banking business carried on within their limits, but we may, as a means of executing our powers over other objects, place that business in the hands of our agents and then declare it exempt from State taxation in their hands. Thus may our own powers and the rights of the States, which we can not directly curtail or invade, be frittered away and extinguished in the use of means employed by us to execute other powers. That a bank of the United States, competent to all the duties which may be required by the Government, might be so organized as not to infringe on our own delegated powers or the reserved rights of the States I do not entertain a doubt. Had the Executive been called upon to furnish the project of such an institution, the duty would have been cheerfully performed. In the absence of such a call it was obviously proper that he should confine himself to pointing out those prominent features in the act presented which in his opinion make it incompatible with the Constitution and sound policy. . . .

The bank is professedly established as an agent of the executive branch of the Government, and its constitutionality is maintained on that ground. Neither upon the propriety of present action nor upon the provisions of this act was the Executive consulted. It has had no opportunity to say that it neither needs nor wants an agent clothed with such powers and favored by such exemptions. There is nothing in its legitimate functions which makes it necessary or proper. Whatever interest or influence, whether public or private, has given birth to this act, it can not be found either in the wishes or necessities of the executive department, by which present action is deemed premature, and the powers conferred upon its agent not only unnecessary, but dangerous to the Government and country.

It is to be regretted that the rich and powerful too often bend the acts of government to their selfish purposes. Distinctions in society will always exist under every just government. Equality of talents, of education, or of wealth can not be produced by human institutions. In the full enjoyment of the gifts of Heaven and the fruits of superior industry, economy, and virtue, every man is equally entitled to protection by law; but when the laws undertake to add to these natural and just advantages artificial distinctions, to grant titles, gratuities, and exclusive privileges, to make the rich richer and the potent more powerful, the humble members of society—the farmers, mechanics, and laborers—who have neither the time nor the means of securing like favors to themselves, have a right to complain of the injustice of their Government. There are no necessary evils in government. Its evils exist only in its abuses. If it would confine itself to equal protection, and as Heaven does its rains, shower its favors alike on the high and the low, the rich and the poor, it would be an unqualified blessing. In the act before me there seems to be a wide and unnecessary departure from these just principles. . . .

Experience should teach us wisdom. Most of the difficulties our Government now encounters and most of the dangers which impend over our Union have sprung from an abandonment of the legitimate objects of Government by our national legislation, and the adoption of such principles as are embodied in this act. Many of our rich men have not been content with equal protection and equal benefits, but have besought us to make them richer by act of Congress. By attempting to gratify their desires we have in the results of our legislation arrayed section against section, interest against interest, and man against man, in a fearful commotion which threatens to shake the foundations of our Union. It is time to pause in our career to review our principles, and if possible revive that devoted patriotism and spirit of compromise which distinguished the sages of the Revolution and the fathers of our Union. If we can not at once, in justice to interests vested under improvident legislation, make our Government what it ought to be, we can at least take a stand against all new grants of monopolies and exclusive privileges, against any prostitution of our Government to the advancement of the few at the expense of the many, and in favor of compromise and gradual reform in our code of laws and system of political economy.

I have now done my duty to my country. If sustained by my fellow-citizens, I shall be grateful and happy; if not, I shall find in the motives which impel me ample grounds for contentment and peace. . . .

ANDREW JACKSON.

FOURTH ANNUAL MESSAGE
December 4, 1832

*Here Jackson recommended reduced protective duties
on the eve of the passage of the Nullification Ordinance
by a convention in South Carolina. He announced the
termination of the public lands as a source of revenue
and further defined his views on internal improvements,
but said little of his continuing conflict with the Bank
of the United States.*

. . . our country presents on every side marks of prosperity and
happiness unequaled, perhaps, in any other portion of the world. . . .

Nor have we less reason to felicitate ourselves on the position of our
political than of our commercial concerns. They remain in the state
in which they were when I last addressed you—a state of prosperity
and peace, the effect of a wise attention to the parting advice of the
revered Father of his Country on this subject, condensed into a maxim
for the use of posterity by one of his most distinguished successors—
to cultivate free commerce and honest friendship with all nations, but
to make entangling alliances with none. A strict adherence to this
policy has kept us aloof from the perplexing questions that now agitate
the European world and have once more deluged those countries with
blood. . . .

I can not too cordially congratulate Congress and my fellow-citizens
on the near approach of that memorable and happy event—the extinction of the public debt of this great and free nation. . . . Within the
four years for which the people have confided the Executive power to
my charge $58,000,000 will have been applied to the payment of the
public debt. . . .

The final removal of this great burthen from our resources affords
the means of further provision for all the objects of general welfare and
public defense which the Constitution authorizes, and presents the
occasion for such further reduction in the revenue as may not be required for them. From the report of the Secretary of the Treasury it will
be seen that after the present year such a reduction may be made. . .
and the subject is earnestly recommended to the consideration of Congress in the hope that the combined wisdom of the representatives
of the people will devise such means of effecting that salutary object
as may remove those burthens which shall be found to fall unequally
upon any and as may promote all the great interests of the community.

Long and patient reflection has strengthened the opinions I have
heretofore expressed to Congress on this subject, and I deem it my

duty on the present occasion again to urge them upon the attention of the Legislature. The soundest maxims of public policy and the principles upon which our republican institutions are founded recommend a proper adaptation of the revenue to the expenditure, and they also require that the expenditure shall be limited to what, by an economical administration, shall be consistent with the simplicity of the Government and necessary to an efficient public service. In effecting this adjustment it is due, in justice to the interests of the different States, and even to the preservation of the Union itself, that the protection afforded by existing laws to any branches of the national industry should not exceed what may be necessary to counteract the regulations of foreign nations and to secure a supply of those articles of manufacture essential to the national independence and safety in time of war. If upon investigation it shall be found, as it is believed it will be, that the legislative protection granted to any particular interest is greater than is indispensably requisite for these objects, I recommend that it be gradually diminished, and that as far as may be consistent with these objects the whole scheme of duties be reduced to the revenue standard as soon as a just regard to the faith of the Government and to the preservation of the large capital invested in establishments of domestic industry will permit.

That manufactures adequate to the supply of our domestic consumption would in the abstract be beneficial to our country there is no reason to doubt, and to effect their establishment there is perhaps no American citizen who would not for awhile be willing to pay a higher price for them. But for this purpose it is presumed that a tariff of high duties, designed for perpetual protection, has entered into the minds of but few of our statesmen. The most they have anticipated is a temporary and, generally, incidential protection, which they maintain has the effect to reduce the price by domestic competition below that of the foreign article. Experience, however, our best guide on this as on other subjects, makes it doubtful whether the advantages of this system are not counterbalanced by many evils, and whether it does not tend to beget in the minds of a large portion of our countrymen a spirit of discontent and jealousy dangerous to the stability of the Union.

What, then, shall be done? Large interests have grown up under the implied pledge of our national legislation, which it would seem a violation of public faith suddenly to abandon. Nothing could justify it but the public safety, which is the supreme law. But those who have vested their capital in manufacturing establishments can not expect that the people will continue permanently to pay high taxes for their benefit, when the money is not required for any legitimate purpose in the administration of the Government. . . .

Those who take an enlarged view of the condition of our country must be satisfied that the policy of protection must be ultimately limited to those articles of domestic manufacture which are indispensable to our safety in time of war. Within this scope, on a reasonable scale, it is recommended by every consideration of patriotism and duty, which will doubtless always secure to it a liberal and efficient support. But beyond this object we have already seen the operation of the system productive of discontent. In some sections of the Republic its influence is deprecated as tending to concentrate wealth into a few hands, and as creating those germs of dependence and vice which in other countries have characterized the existence of monopolies and proved so destructive of liberty and the general good. A large portion of the people in one section of the Republic declares it not only inexpedient on these grounds, but as disturbing the equal relations of property by legislation, and therefore unconstitutional and unjust. . . .

It is my painful duty to state that in one quarter of the United States opposition to the revenue laws has arisen to a height which threatens to thwart their execution, if not to endanger the integrity of the Union. Whatever obstructions may be thrown in the way of the judicial authorities of the General Government, it is hoped they will be able peaceably to overcome them by the prudence of their own officers and the patriotism of the people. But should this reasonable reliance on the moderation and good sense of all portions of our fellow-citizens be disappointed, it is believed that the laws themselves are fully adequate to the suppression of such attempts as may be immediately made. Should the exigency arise rendering the execution of the existing laws impracticable from any cause whatever, prompt notice of it will be given to Congress, with a suggestion of such views and measures as may be deemed necessary to meet it. . . .

It is my duty to acquaint you with an arrangement made by the Bank of the United States with a portion of the holders of the 3 per cent stock, by which the Government will be deprived of the use of the public funds longer than was anticipated. . . . An inquiry into the transactions of the institution, embracing the branches as well as the principal bank, seems called for by the credit which is given throughout the country to many serious charges impeaching its character, and which if true may justly excite the apprehension that it is no longer a safe depository of the money of the people.

Among the interests which merit the consideration of Congress after the payment of the public debt, one of the most important, in my view, is that of the public lands. . . .

It can not be doubted that the speedy settlement of these lands constitutes the true interest of the Republic. The wealth and strength of a country are its population, and the best part of that population are the cultivators of the soil. Independent farmers are everywhere the basis of society and true friends of liberty. . . .

It seems to me to be our true policy that the public lands shall cease as soon as practicable to be a source of revenue, and that they be sold to settlers in limited parcels at a price barely sufficient to reimburse to the United States the expense of the present system and the cost arising under our Indian compacts. . . .

In former messages I have expressed my conviction that the Constitution does not warrant the application of the funds of the General Government to objects of internal improvement which are not national in their character, and, both as a means of doing justice to all interests and putting an end to a course of legislation calculated to destroy the purity of the Government, have urged the necessity of reducing the whole subject to some fixed and certain rule. . . .

Without some general and well-defined principles ascertaining those objects of internal improvement to which the means of the nation may be constitutionally applied, it is obvious that the exercise of the power can never be satisfactory. Besides the danger to which it exposes Congress of making hasty appropriations to works of the character of which they may be frequently ignorant, it promotes a mischievous and corrupting influence upon elections by holding out to the people the fallacious hope that the success of a certain candidate will make navigable their neighboring creek or river, bring commerce to their doors, and increase the value of their property. It thus favors combinations to squander the treasure of the country upon a multitude of local objects, as fatal to just legislation as to the purity of public men.

If a system compatible with the Constitution can not be devised which is free from such tendencies, we should recollect that that instrument provides within itself the mode of its amendment, and that there is, therefore, no excuse for the assumption of doubtful powers by the General Government. . . .

Being impressed with the conviction that the extension of the power to make internal improvements beyond the limit I have suggested, even if it be deemed constitutional, is subversive of the best interests of our country, I earnestly recommend to Congress to refrain from its exercise in doubtful cases, except in relation to improvements already begun, unless they shall first procure from the States such an amendment of the Constitution as will define its character and prescribe its bounds. If the States feel themselves competent to these objects, why should this Government wish to assume the power? If they do not, then they will not hesitate to make the grant. Both Governments are the Governments of the people; improvements must be made with the money of the people, and if the money can be collected and applied by those more simple and economical political machines, the State Governments, it will unquestionably be safer and better for the people than to add to the splendor, the patronage, and the power of the General Government....

I am happy to inform you that the wise and humane policy of transferring from the eastern to the western side of the Mississippi the remnants of our aboriginal tribes, with their own consent and upon just terms, has been steadily pursued, and is approaching, I trust, its consummation. . . .

With that portion of the Cherokees, however, living within the State of Georgia it has been found impracticable as yet to make a satisfactory adjustment. Such was my anxiety to remove all the grounds of complaint and to bring to a termination the difficulties in which they are involved that I directed the very liberal propositions to be made to them. . .An ample indemnity was offered for their present possessions, a liberal provision for their future support and improvement, and full security for their private and political rights. Whatever difference of opinion may have prevailed respecting the just claims of these people, there will probably be none respecting the liberality of the propositions, and very little respecting the expediency of their immediate acceptance. They were, however, rejected. . . .

We should bear constantly in mind the fact that the considerations which induced the framers of the Constitution to withhold from the General Government the power to regulate the great mass of the business and concerns of the people have been fully justified by experience, and that it can not now be doubted that the genius of all our institutions prescribes simplicity and economy as the characteristics of the reform which is yet to be effected in the present and future execution of the functions bestowed upon us by the Constitution.

Limited to a general superintending power to maintain peace at home and abroad, and to prescribe laws on a few subjects of general interest not calculated to restrict human liberty, but to enforce human rights, this Government will find its strength and its glory in the faithful discharge of these plain and simple duties. Relieved by its protecting shield from the fear of war and the apprehension of oppression, the free enterprise of our citizens, aided by the State sovereignties, will work out improvements and ameliorations which can not fail to demonstrate that the great truth that the people can govern themselves is not only realized in our example, but that it is done by a machinery in government so simple and economical as scarcely to be felt. That the Almighty Ruler of the Universe may so direct our deliberations and overrule our acts as to make us instrumental in securing a result so dear to mankind is my most earnest and sincere prayer.

ANDREW JACKSON.

THE PROCLAMATION TO THE
PEOPLE OF SOUTH CAROLINA
December 10, 1832

*The South Carolina Ordinance of Nullification of No-
vember 24, 1832 nullified the tariffs of 1828 and 1832
using theories advanced by John C. Calhoun in his
South Carolina Exposition of 1828 and his "Fort Hill
Address" of 1831. In perhaps Jackson's finest hour as
President, he responded with a strong proclamation
which denied a constitutional authority for nullification
and affirmed his intent to uphold the laws, but was
conciliatory in tone. He sought Congressional action
in his message of January 16, 1833, resulting in the
enactment of the Force Bill.*

PROCLAMATION.
By Andrew Jackson, President of the United States.

Whereas a convention assembled in the State of South Carolina have
passed an ordinance by which they declare "that the several acts and
parts of acts of the Congress of the United States purporting to be laws
for the imposing of duties and imposts on the importation of foreign
commodities, and now having actual operation and effect within the
United States, and more especially" two acts for the same purposes
passed on the 29th of May, 1828, and on the 14th of July, 1832, "are
unauthorized by the Constitution of the United States, and violate the
true meaning and intent thereof, and are null and void and no law,"
nor binding on the citizens of that State or its officers; and by the
said ordinance it is further declared to be unlawful for any of the
constituted authorities of the State or of the United States to enforce
the payment of the duties imposed by the said acts within the same
State, and that it is the duty of the legislature to pass such laws as
may be necessary to give full effect to the said ordinance; and

Whereas by the said ordinance it is further ordained that in no case
of law or equity decided in the courts of said State wherein shall be
drawn in question the validity of the said ordinance, or of the acts
of the legislature that may be passed to give it effect, or of the said
laws of the United States, no appeal shall be allowed to the Supreme
Court of the United States, nor shall any copy of the record be permitted or allowed for that purpose, and that any person attempting to
take such appeal shall be punished as for contempt of court; and,
finally, the said ordinance declares that the people of South Carolina
will maintain the said ordinance at every hazard, and that they will

consider the passage of any act by Congress abolishing or closing the ports of the said State . . . or any other act of the Federal Government to coerce the State, . . . or to enforce the said acts otherwise than through the civil tribunals of the country, as inconsistent with the longer continuance of South Carolina in the Union, and that the people of the said State will thenceforth hold themselves absolved from all further obligation to maintain or preserve their political connection with the people of the other States, and will forthwith proceed to organize a separate government and do all other acts and things which sovereign and independent states may of right do; and

Whereas the said ordinance prescribes to the people of South Carolina a course of conduct in direct violation of their duty as citizens of the United States, contrary to the laws of their country, subversive of its Constitution, and having for its object the destruction of the Union—. . .

To preserve this bond of our political existence from destruction, to maintain inviolate this state of national honor and prosperity, and to justify the confidence my fellow-citizens have reposed in me, I, Andrew Jackson, President of the United States, have thought proper to issue this my proclamation, stating my views of the Constitution and laws applicable to the measures adopted by the convention of South Carolina and to the reasons they have put forth to sustain them, declaring the course which duty will require me to pursue, and, appealing to the understanding and patriotism of the people, warn them of the consequences that must inevitably result from an observance of the dictates of the convention.

Strict duty would require of me nothing more than the exercise of those powers with which I am now or may hereafter be invested for preserving the peace of the Union and for the execution of the laws; but the imposing aspect which opposition has assumed in this case, by clothing itself with State authority, and the deep interest which the people of the United States must all feel in preventing a resort to stronger measures while there is a hope that anything will be yielded to reasoning and remonstrance, perhaps demand, and will certainly justify, a full exposition to South Carolina and the nation of the views I entertain of this important question, as well as a distinct enunciation of the course which my sense of duty will require me to pursue.

The ordinance is founded, not on the indefeasible right of resisting acts which are plainly unconstitutional and too oppressive to be endured, but on the strange position that any one State may not only declare an act of Congress void, but prohibit its execution; that they may do this consistently with the Constitution; that the true construction of that instrument permits a State to retain its place in the Union and yet be bound by no other of its laws than those it may choose to consider as constitutional. It is true, they add, that to justify this abrogation of a law it must be palpably contrary to the Constitution; but it is evident that to give the right of resisting laws of that description, coupled with the uncontrolled right to decide what laws deserve that character, is to give the power of resisting all laws; for as by the theory there is no appeal, the reasons alleged by the State, good or bad, must prevail. If it should be said that public opinion is a sufficient check against the abuse of this power, it may be asked why it is not deemed a sufficient guard against the passage of an unconstitutional act by Congress? There is, however, a restraint in this last case which makes the assumed power of a State more indefensible, and which does not exist in the other. There are two appeals from an unconstitutional act passed by Congress—one to the judiciary, the other to the people and the States. There is no appeal from the State decision in theory, and the practical illustration shows that the courts are closed against an application to review it, both judges and jurors being sworn to decide in its favor. But reasoning on this subject is superfluous when our social compact, in express terms, declares that the laws of the United States, its Constitution, and treaties made under it are the supreme law of the land, and, for greater caution, adds "that the judges in every State shall be bound thereby, anything in the constitution or laws of any State to the contrary notwithstanding." And it may be asserted without fear of refutation that no federative government could exist without a similar provision. Look for a moment to the consequence. If South Carolina considers the revenue laws unconstitutional and has a right to prevent their execution in the port of Charleston, there would be a clear constitutional objection to their collection in every other port; and no revenue could be collected anywhere, for all imposts must be equal. It is no answer to repeat that an unconstitutional law is no law so long as the question of its legality is to be decided by the State itself, for every law operating injuriously upon any local interest will be perhaps thought, and certainly represented, as unconstitutional, and, as has been shown, there is no appeal.

If this doctrine had been established at an earlier day, the Union would have been dissolved in its infancy. The excise law in Pennsylvania, the embargo and nonintercourse law in the Eastern States, the carriage tax in Virginia, were all deemed unconstitutional, and were more unequal in their operation than any of the laws now complained of; but, fortunately, none of those States discovered that they had the right now claimed by South Carolina. The war into which we were forced to support the dignity of the nation and the rights of our

citizens might have ended in defeat and disgrace, instead of victory
and honor, if the States who supposed it a ruinous and unconstitutional measure had thought they possessed the right of nullifying the
act by which it was declared and denying supplies for its prosecution.
Hardly and unequally as those measures bore upon several members
of the Union, to the legislatures of none did this efficient and peacable
remedy, as it is called, suggest itself. The discovery of this important
feature in our Constitution was reserved to the present day. To the
statesmen of South Carolina belongs the invention, and upon the
citizens of that State will unfortunately fall the evils of reducing it
to practice.

If the doctrine of a State veto upon the laws of the Union carries
with it internal evidence of its impracticable absurdity, our constitutional history will also afford abundant proof that it would have been
repudiated with indignation had it been proposed to form a feature
in our Government. . . .

. . .our present happy Constitution was formed. . .for important
objects that are announced in the preamble, made in the name and
by the authority of the people of the United States, whose delegates
framed and whose conventions approved it. The most important among
these objects—that which is placed first in rank, on which all the
others rest—is "to form a more perfect union." Now, is it possible
that even if there were no express provision giving supremacy to the
Constitution and laws of the United States over those of the States,
can it be conceived that an instrument made for the purpose of "forming a more perfect union" than that of the Confederation could be so
constructed by the assembled wisdom of our country as to substitute
for that Confederation a form of government dependent for its existence on the local interest, the party spirit, of a State, or of a prevailing faction in a State? Every man of plain, unsophisticated understanding who hears the question will give such an answer as will preserve the Union. Metaphysical subtlety, in pursuit of an impracticable
theory, could alone have devised one that is calculated to destroy it.

I consider, then, the power to annul a law of the United States,
assumed by one State, incompatible with the existence of the Union,
contradicted expressly by the letter of the Constitution, unauthorized
by its spirit, inconsistent with every principle on which it was founded, and destructive of the great object for which it was formed.

After this general view of the leading principle, we must examine
the particular application of it which is made in the ordinance.

The preamble rests its justification on these grounds: It assumes as
a fact that the obnoxious laws, although they purport to be laws for
raising revenue, were in reality intended for the protection of man-

ufactures, which purpose it asserts to be unconstitutional; that the operation of these laws is unequal; that the amount raised by them is greater than is required by the wants of the Government; and, finally, that the proceeds are to be applied to objects unauthorized by the Constituion. These are the only causes alleged to justify an open opposition to the laws of the country and a threat of seceding from the Union if any attempt should be made to enforce them. The first virtually acknowledges that the law in question was passed under a power expressly given by the Constitution to lay and collect imposts; but its constitutionality is drawn in question from the motives of those who passed it. However apparent this purpose may be in the present case, nothing can be more dangerous than to admit the position that an unconstitutional purpose entertained by the members who assent to a law enacted under a constitutional power shall make that law void. For how is that purpose to be ascertained? Who is to make the scrutiny? How often may bad purposes be falsely imputed, in how many cases are they concealed by false professions, in how many is no declaration of motive made? Admit this doctrine, and you give to the States an uncontrolled right to decide, and every law may be annulled under this pretext. If, therefore, the absurd and dangerous doctrine should be admitted that a State may annul an unconstitutional law, or one that it deems such, it will not apply to the present case.

The next objection is that the laws in question operate unequally. This objection may be made with truth to every law that has been or can be passed. The wisdom of man never yet contrived a system of taxation that would operate with perfect equality. If the unequal operation of a law makes it unconstitutional, and if all laws of that description may be abrogated by any State for that cause, then, indeed, is the Federal Constitution unworthy of the slightest effort for its preservation. . . .Nor did the States, when they severally ratified it, do so under the impression that a veto on the laws of the United States was reserved to them or that they could exercise it by implication. Search the debates in all their conventions, examine the speeches of the most zealous opposers of Federal authority, look at the amendments that were proposed; they are all silent—not a syllable uttered, not a vote given, not a motion made to correct the explicit supremacy given to the laws of the Union over those of the States, or to show that implication, as is now contended, could defeat it. No; we have not erred. The Constitution is still the object of our reverence, the bond of our Union, our defense in danger, the source of our prosperity in peace. It shall descend, as we have received it, uncorrupted by sophistical construction, to our posterity; and the sacrifices of local interest, of State prejudices, of personal animosities, that were made to bring it into existence, will again be patriotically offered for its support.

The two remaining objections made by the ordinance to these laws are that the sums intended to be raised by them are greater than are required and that the proceeds will be unconstitutionally employed.

The Constitution has given, expressly, to Congress the right of raising revenue and of determining the sum the public exigencies will require. The States have no control over the exercise of this right other than that which results from the power of changing the representatives who abuse it, and thus procure redress. . . .

The ordinance, with the same knowledge of the future that characterizes a former objection, tells you that the proceeds of the tax will be unconstitutionally applied. If this could be ascertained with certainty, the objection would with more propriety be reserved for the law so applying the proceeds, but surely can not be urged against the laws levying the duty.

These are the allegations contained in the ordinance. Examine them seriously, my fellow-citizens; judge for youselves. I appeal to you to determine whether they are so clear, so convincing, as to leave no doubt of their correctness; and even if you should come to this conclusion, how far they justify the reckless, destructive course which you are directed to pursue. Review these objections and the conclusions drawn from them once more. What are they? Every law, then, for raising revenue, according to the South Carolina ordinance, may be rightfully annulled, unless it be so framed as no law ever will or can be framed. Congress have a right to pass laws for raising revenue and each State have a right to oppose their execution—two rights directly opposed to each other; and yet is this absurdity supposed to be contained in an instrument drawn for the express purpose of avoiding collisions between the States and the General Government by an assembly of the most enlightened statesmen and purest patriots ever embodied for a similar purpose.

In vain have these sages declared that Congress shall have power to lay and collect taxes, duties, imposts, and excises; in vain have they provided that they shall have power to pass laws which shall be necessary and proper to carry those powers into execution, that those laws and that Constitution shall be the "supreme law of the land, and that the judges in every State shall be bound thereby, anything in the constitution or laws of any State to the contrary notwithstanding;". . .if a bare majority of the voters in any one State may, on a real or supposed knowledge of the intent with which a law has been passed, declare themselves free from its operation; say, here it gives too little, there, too much, and operates unequally; here it suffers articles to be free that ought to be taxed; there it taxes those that ought to be free; in this case the proceeds are intended to be applied to purposes which we do not approve; in that, the amount raised is more than is wanted. . . .

The Constitution declares that the judicial powers of the United States extend to cases arising under the laws of the United States, and that such laws, the Constitution, and treaties shall be paramount to the State constitutions and laws. The judiciary act prescribes the mode by which the case may be brought before a court of the United States by appeal when a State tribunal shall decide against this provision of the Constitution. The ordinance declares there shall be no appeal—makes the State law paramount to the Constitution and laws of the United States, forces judges and jurors to swear that they will disregard their provisions, and even makes it penal in a suitor to attempt relief by appeal. It further declares that it shall not be lawful for the authorities of the United States or of that State to enforce the payment of duties imposed by the revenue laws within its limits.

Here is a law of the United States, not even pretended to be unconstitutional, repealed by the authority of a small majority of the voters of a single State. Here is a provision of the Constitution which is solemnly abrogated by the same authority.

On such expositions and reasonings the ordinance grounds not only an assertion of the right to annul the laws of which it complains, but to enforce it by a threat of seceding from the Union if any attempt is made to execute them.

This right to secede is deduced from the nature of the Constitution, which, they say, is a compact between sovereign States who have preserved their whole sovereignty and therefore are subject to no superior; that because they made the compact they can break it when in their opinion it has been departed from by the other States. Fallacious as this course of reasoning is, it enlists State pride and finds advocates in the honest prejudices of those who have not studied the nature of our Government sufficiently to see the radical error on which it rests. . . .

The Constitution of the United States, then, forms a government, not a league; and whether it be formed by compact between the States or in any other manner, its character is the same. It is a Government in which all the people are represented, which operates directly on the people individually, not upon the States; they retained all the power they did not grant. But each State, having expressly parted with so many powers as to constitute, jointly with the other States, a single nation, can not, from that period, possess any right to secede, because such secession does not break a league, but destroys the unity of a nation; and any injury to the unity is not only a breach which would result from the contravention of a compact, but it is an offense against the whole Union. To say that any State may at pleasure secede from the Union is to say that the United States are not a nation, because it would be a solecism to contend that any part of a nation might dissolve its connection with the other parts, to their injury or ruin, without committing any offense. Secession, like any other revolutionary act, may be morally justified by the extremity of oppression; but to call it a constitutional right is confounding the meaning of terms, and can only be done through gross error or to deceive those who are willing to assert a right, but would pause before they made a revolution or incur the penalties consequent on a failure.

Because the Union was formed by a compact, it is said the parties to that compact may, when they feel themselves aggrieved, depart from it; but it is precisely because it is a compact that they can not. A compact is an agreement or binding obligation. It may by its terms have a sanction or penalty for its breach, or it may not. If it contains no sanction, it may be broken with no other consequence than moral guilt; if it have a sanction, then the breach incurs the designated or implied penalty. A league between independent nations generally has no sanction other than a moral one; or if it should contain a penalty, as there is no common superior it can not be enforced. A government, on the contrary, always has a sanction, express or implied; and in our case it is both necessarily implied and expressly given. An attempt, by force of arms, to destroy a government is an offense, by whatever means the constitutional compact may have been formed; and such government has the right by the law of self-defense to pass acts for punishing the offender, unless that right is modified, restrained, or resumed by the constitutional act. In our system, although it is modified in the case of treason, yet authority is expressly given to pass all laws necessary to carry its powers into effect, and under this grant provision has been made for punishing acts which obstruct the due administration of the laws.

It would seem superfluous to add anything to show the nature of that union which connects us, but as erroneous opinions on this subject are the foundation of doctrines the most destructive to our peace, I must give some further development to my views on this subject. No one, fellow-citizens, has a higher reverence for the reserved rights of the States than the Magistrate who now addresses you. No one would make greater personal sacrifices or official exertions to defend them from violation; but equal care must be taken to prevent, on their part, an improper interference with or resumption of the rights they have vested in the nation. The line has not been so distinctly drawn as to avoid doubts in some cases of the exercise of power. Men of the best intentions and soundest views may differ in their construction of some parts of the Constitution; but there are others on which dispassionate reflection can leave no doubt. Of this nature appears to be the assumed right of secession. It rests, as we have seen, on the alleged undivided sovereignty of the States and on their having formed in this sovereign capacity a compact which is called the Constitution, from which, because they made it, they have the right to secede. Both of these positions are erroneous, and some of the arguments to prove them so have been anticipated.

The States severally have not retained their entire sovereignty. It has been shown that in becoming parts of a nation, not members of a league, they surrendered many of their essential parts of sovereignty. The right to make treaties, declare war, levy taxes, exercise exclusive judicial and legislative powers, were all of them functions of sovereign power. The States, then, for all these important purposes were no longer sovereign. The allegiance of their citizens was transferred, in the first instance, to the Government of the United States; they became American citizens and owed obedience to the Constitution of the United States and to laws made in conformity with the powers it vested in Congress. This last position has not been and can not be denied . . . The unity of our political character (as has been shown for another purpose) commenced with its very existence. Under the royal Government we had no separate character; our opposition to its oppressions began as united colonies. We were the United States under the Confederation, and the name was perpetuated and the Union rendered more perfect by the Federal Constitution. In none of these stages did we consider ourselves in any other light than as forming one nation. Treaties and alliances were made in the name of all. Troops were raised for the joint defense. How, then, with all these proofs that under all changes of our position we had, for designated purposes and with defined powers, created national governments, how is is that the most perfect of those several modes of union should now be considered as a mere league that may be dissolved at pleasure? It is from an abuse of terms. Compact is used as synonymous with league, although the true term is not employed, because it would at once show the fallacy of the reasoning. It would not do to say that our Constitution was only a league, but it is labored to prove it a compact (which in one sense it is) and then to argue that as a league is a compact every compact between nations must of course be a league, and that from such an engagement every sovereign power has a right to recede. But it has been shown that in this sense the States are not sovereign, and that even if they were, and the national Constitution had been formed by compact, there would be no right in any one State to exonerate itself from its obligations. . . .

This, then, is the position in which we stand: A small majority of the citizens of one State in the Union have elected delegates to a State convention; that convention has ordained that all the revenue laws of the United States must be repealed, or that they are no longer a member of the Union. The governor of that State has recommended to the legislature the raising of an army to carry the secession into effect, and that he may be empowered to give clearances to vessels in the name of the State. No act of violent opposition to the laws has yet been committed, but such a state of things is hourly apprehended. And it is the intent of this instrument to proclaim, not only that the duty imposed on me by the Constitution "to take care that the laws be faithfully executed" shall be performed to the extent of the powers already vested in me by law, or of such others as the wisdom of Congress shall devise and intrust to me for that purpose, but to warn the citizens of South Carolina who have been deluded into an opposition to the laws of the danger they will incur by obedience to the illegal and disorganizing ordinance of the convention; to exhort those who have refused to support it to persevere in their determination to uphold the Constitution and laws of their country; and to point out to all the perilous situation into which the good people of that State have been led, and that the course they are urged to pursue is one of ruin and disgrace to the very State whose rights they affect to support.

Fellow-citizens of my native State, let me not only admonish you, as the First Magistrate of our common country, not to incur the penalty of its laws, but use the influence that a father would over his children whom he saw rushing to certain ruin. In that paternal language, with that paternal feeling, let me tell you, my countrymen, that you are deluded by men who are either deceived themselves or wish to deceive you. . . .They are not champions of liberty, emulating the fame of our Revolutionary fathers, nor are you an oppressed people, contending, as they repeat to you, against worse than colonial vassalage. You are free members of a flourishing and happy Union. There is no settled design to oppress you. You have indeed felt the unequal operation of laws which may have been unwisely, not unconstitutionally, passed; but that inequality must necessarily be removed. At the very moment when you were madly urged on to the unfortunate course you have begun a change in public opinion had commenced. The nearly approaching payment of the public debt and the consequent necessity of a diminution of duties had already produced a considerable reduction, and that, too, on some articles of general consumption in your State. The importance of this change was underrated, and you were authoritatively told that no further alleviation of your burthens was to be expected at the very time when the condition of the country imperiously demanded such a modification of the duties as should reduce them to a just and equitable scale. But, as if apprehensive of the effect of this change in allaying your discontents, you were precipitated into the fearful state in which you now find yourselves. . . .

For what would you exchange your share in the advantages and honor of the Union? For the dream of a separate independence—a dream interrupted by bloody conflicts with your neighbors and a vile dependence on a foreign power. If your leaders could succeed in establishing a separation, what would be your situation? Are you united at home? Are you free from the apprehension of civil discord, wih all its fearful consequences? Do our neighboring republics, every day suffering some new revolution or contending with some new insurrection, do they excite your envy? But the dictates of a high duty oblige me solemnly to announce that you can not succeed. The laws of the United States must be executed. I have no discretionary power on the subject; my duty is emphatically pronounced in the Constitution. Those who told you that you might peaceably prevent their execution deceived you; they could not have been deceived themselves. They know that a forcible opposition could alone prevent the execution of the laws, and they know that such opposition must be repelled. Their object is disunion. But be not deceived by names. Disunion by armed force is treason. Are you really ready to incur its guilt? If you are, on the heads of the instigators of the act be the dreadful consequences; on their heads be the dishonor, but on yours may fall the punishment. On your unhappy State will inevitably fall all the evils of the conflict you force upon the Government of your country. It can not accede to the mad project of disunion, of which you would be the first victims. Its First Magistrate can not, if he would, avoid the performance of his duty. The consequence must be fearful for you, distressing to your fellow-citizens here and to the friends of good government throughout the world. Its enemies have beheld our prosperity with a vexation they could not conceal; it was a standing refutation of their slavish doctrines, and they will point to our discord with the triump of malignant joy. It is yet in your power to disappoint them. . . .

Fellow-citizens of the United States, the threat of unhallowed disunion, the names of those once respected by whom it is uttered, the array of military force to support it, denote the approach of a crisis in our affairs on which the continuance of our unexampled prosperity, our political existence, and perhaps that of all free government may depend. The conjuncture demanded a free, a full, and explicit enunciation, not only of my intentions, but of my principles of action; and as the claim was asserted of a right by a State to annul the laws of the Union, and even to secede from it at pleasure, a frank exposition of my opinions in relation to the origin and form of our Government and the construction I give to the instrument by which it was created seemed to be proper. Having the fullest confidence in the justness of the legal and constitutional opinion of my duties which has been expressed, I rely with equal confidence on your undivided support in my determination to execute the laws, to preserve the Union by all constitutional means, to arrest, if possible, by moderate and firm measures the necessity of a recourse to force; and if it be the will of Heaven that the recurrence of its primeval curse on man for the shedding of a brothers blood should fall upon our land, that it be not called down by any offensive act on the part of the United States.

Fellow-citizens, the momentous case is before you. On your undivided support of your Government depends the decision of the great question it involves—whether your sacred Union will be preserved and the blessing it secures to us as one people shall be perpetuated. No one can doubt that the unanimity with which that decision will be expressed will be such as to inspire new confidence in republican institutions, and that the prudence, the wisdom, and the courage which it will bring to their defense will transmit them unimpaired and invigorated to our children.

May the Great Ruler of Nations grant that the signal blessings with which He has favored ours may not, by the madness of party or personal ambition, be disregarded and lost; and may His wise providence bring those who have produced this crisis to see the folly before they feel the misery of civil strife, and inspire a returning veneration for that Union which, if we may dare to penetrate His designs, He has chosen as the only means of attaining the high destinies to which we may reasonably aspire.

ANDREW JACKSON.

SECOND INAUGURAL ADDRESS
March 4, 1833

In contrat to the inauguration of Jackson's first term as President, that of his second term was marked by great simplicity. The oath of office was taken in the House chamber while snow covered the ground outside. Directing his Second Inaugural Address to the South Carolina nullification crisis, Jackson defended the rights of the states and took a narrow view of the powers of the national government, but pledged his determination to insure the preservation of the Union.

FELLOW—CITIZENS: The will of the American people, expressed through their unsolicited suffrages, calls me before you to pass through the solemnities preparatory to taking upon myself the duties of President of the United States for another term. For their approbation of my public conduct through a period which has not been without its difficulties, and for this renewed expression of their confidence in my good intentions, I am at a loss for terms adequate to the expression of my gratitude. It shall be displayed to the extent of my humble abilities in continued efforts so to administer the Government as to preserve their liberty and promote their happiness.

So many events have occurred within the last four years which have necessarily called forth — sometimes under circumstances the most delicate and painful—my views of the principles and policy which ought to be pursued by the General Government that I need on this occasion but allude to a few leading considerations connected with some of them.

The foreign policy adopted by our Government soon after the formation of our present Constitution, and very generally pursued by successive Administrations, has been crowned with almost complete success, and has elevated our character among the nations of the earth. To do justice to all and to submit to wrong from none has been during my Administration its governing maxim, and so happy have been its results that we are not only at peace with all the world, but have few causes of controversy, and those of minor importance, remaining unadjusted.

In the domestic policy of this Government there are two objects which especially deserve the attention of the people and their representatives, and which have been and will continue to be the subjects of my increasing solicitude. They are the preservation of the rights of the several States and the integrity of the Union.

These great objects are necessarily connected, and can only be attained by an enlightened exercise of the powers of each within its appropriate sphere in conformity with the public will constitutionally expressed. To this end it becomes the duty of all to yield a ready and patriotic submission to the laws constitutionally enacted, and thereby promote and strengthen a proper confidence in those institutions of the several States and of the United States which the people themselves have ordained for their own government.

My experience in public concerns and the observation of a life somewhat advanced confirm the opinions long since imbibed by me, that the destruction of our State governments or the annihilation of their control over the local concerns of the people would lead directly to revolution and anarchy, and finally to despotism and military domination. In proportion, therefore, as the General Government encroaches upon the rights of the States, in the same proportion does it impair its own power and detract from its ability to fulfill the purposes of its creation. Solemnly impressed with these considerations, my countrymen will ever find me ready to exercise my constitutional powers in arresting measures which may directly or indirectly encroach upon the rights of the States or tend to consolidate all political power in the General Government. But of equal, and, indeed, of incalculable, importance is the union of these States and the sacred duty of all to contribute to its preservation by a liberal support of the General Government in the exercise of its just powers. You have been wisely admonished to "accustom yourselves to think and speak of the Union as of the palladium of your political safety and prosperity, watching for its preservation with jealous anxiety, discountenancing whatever may suggest even a suspicion that it can in any event be abandoned, and indignantly frowning upon the first dawning of any attempt to alienate any portion of our country from the rest or to enfeeble the sacred ties which now link together the various parts." Without union our independence and liberty would never have been achieved; without union they never can be maintained. Divided into twenty-four, or even a smaller number, of separate communities, we shall see our internal trade burdened with numberless restraints and exactions; communication between distant points and sections obstructed or cut off; our sons made soldiers to deluge with blood the fields they now till in peace; the mass of our people borne down and impoverished by taxes to support armies and navies, and military leaders at the head of their victorious legions becoming our lawgivers and judges. The loss of liberty, of all good government, of peace, plenty, and happiness, must inevitably follow a dissolution of the Union. In supporting it, therefore, we support all that is dear to the freeman and the philanthropist.

The time at which I stand before you is full of interest. The eyes of all nations are fixed on our Republic. The event of the existing crisis will be decisive in the opinion of mankind of the practicability of our federal system of government. Great is the stake placed in our hands; great is the responsiblity which must rest upon the people of the United States. Let us realize the importance of the attitude in which we stand before the world. Let us exercise forbearance and firmness. Let us extricate our country from the dangers which surround it and learn wisdom from the lessons they inculcate.

Deeply impressed with the truth of these observations, and under the obligation of that solemn oath which I am about to take, I shall continue to exert all my faculties to maintain the just powers of the Constitution and to transmit unimpaired to posterity the blessings of our Federal Union. At the same time, it will be my aim to inculcate by my official acts the necessity of exercising by the General Government those powers only that are clearly delegated; to encourage simplicity and economy in the expenditures of the Government; to raise no more money from the people than may be requisite for these objects, and in a manner that will best promote the interests of all classes of the community and of all portions of the Union. Constantly bearing in mind that in entering into society "individuals must give up a share of liberty to preserve the rest," it will be my desire so to discharge my duties as to foster with our brethren in all parts of the country a spirit of liberal concession and compromise, and, by reconciling our fellow-citizens to those partial sacrifices which they must unavoidably make for the preservation of a greater good, to recommend our invaluable Government and Union to the confidence and affections of the American people.

Finally, it is my most fervent prayer to that Almighty Being before whom I now stand, and who has kept us in His hands from the infancy of our Republic to the present day, that He will so overrule all my intentions and actions and inspire the hearts of my fellow-citizens that we may be preserved from dangers of all kinds and continue forever a united and happy people.

THE REMOVAL OF THE PUBLIC DEPOSITS
Read to the Cabinet September 18, 1833

Jackson saw his reelection in 1832 as a popular referendum on his veto of the bank bill. To defeat Nicholas Biddle's renewed efforts to secure the recharter of the bank, Jackson urged his divided Cabinet to support his decision to remove the public deposits to state banks and at the same time he defined the responsibility of the Secretary of the Treasury. Later he removed Secretary Duane when he declined to comply and appointed Roger B. Taney who carried out the removal of the deposits September 26, 1833.

Having carefully and anxiously considered all the facts and arguments which have been submitted to him relative to a removal of the public deposits from the Bank of the United States, the President deems it his duty to communicate in this manner to his Cabinet the final conclusions of his own mind and the reasons on which they are founded, in order to put them in durable form and to prevent misconceptions. . . .

Whatever may be the opinions of others, the President considers his reelection as a decision of the people against the bank. In the concluding paragraph of his veto message he said:

I have now done my duty to my country. If sustained by my fellow-citizens, I shall be grateful and happy; if not, I shall find in the motives which impel me ample grounds for contentment and peace.

He was sustained by a just people, and he desires to evince his gratitude by carrying into effect their decision so far as it depends upon him. . . .

On the whole, the President considers it as conclusively settled that the charter of the Bank of the United States will not be renewed, and he has no reasonable ground to believe that any substitute will be established. Being bound to regulate his course by the laws as they exist, and not to anticipate the interference of the legislative power for the purpose of framing new systems, it is proper for him seasonably to consider the means by which the services rendered by the Bank of the United States are to be performed after its charter shall expire.

The existing laws declare that—

"The deposits of the money of the United States in places in which the said bank and branches thereof may be established shall be made in said bank or branches thereof unless the Secretary of the Treasury shall at any time otherwise order and direct, in which case the Secretary of the Treasury shall immediately lay before Congress, if in session, and, if not, immediately after the commencement of the next session, the reasons of such order or direction."

The power of the Secretary of the Treasury over the deposits is unqualified. The provision that he shall report his reasons to Congress is no limitation. Had it not been inserted he would have been responsible to Congress had he made a removal for any other than good reasons, and his responsibility now ceases upon the rendition of sufficient ones to Congress. The only object of the provision is to make his reasons accessible to Congress and enable that body the more readily to judge of their soundness and purity, and thereupon to make such further provision by law as the legislative power may think proper in relation to the deposit of the public money. . . .

And it is a matter of surprise that a power which in the infancy of the bank was freely asserted as one of the ordinary and familiar duties of the Secretary of the Treasury should now be gravely questioned, and attempts made to excite and alarm the public mind as if some new and unheard-of power was about to be usurped by the executive branch of the Government.

It is but a little more than two and a half years to the termination of the charter of the present bank. It is considered as the decision of the country that it shall then cease to exist, and no man, the President believes, has reasonable ground for expectation that any other Bank of the United States will be created by Congress.

To the Treasury Department is intrusted the safe-keeping and faithful application of the public moneys. A plan of collection different from the present must therefore be introduced and put in complete operation before the dissolution of the present bank. When shall it be commenced? Shall no step be taken in this essential concern until the charter expires and the Treasury finds itself without an agent, its accounts in confusion, with no depository for its funds, and the whole business of the Government deranged, or shall it be delayed until six months, or a year, or two years before the expiration of the charter? It is obvious that any new system which may be substituted in the place of the Bank of the United States could not be suddenly carried into effect on the termination of its existence without serious inconvenience to the Government and the people. Its vast amount of notes are then to be redeemed and withdrawn from circulation and its immense debt collected. These operations must be gradual, otherwise much suffering and distress will be brought upon the community.

It ought to be not a work of months only, but of years, and the President thinks it can not, with due attention to the interests of the people, be longer postponed. It is safer to begin it too soon than to delay it too long. . . .

But as the President presumes that the charter to the bank is to be considered as a contract on the part of the Government, it is not now in the power of Congress to disregard its stipulations; and by the terms of that contract the public money is to be deposited in the bank during the continuance of its charter unless the Secretary of the Treasury shall otherwise direct. Unless, therefore, the Secretary of the Treasury first acts, Congress have no power on the subject, for they can not add a new clause to the charter or strike one out of it without the consent of the bank, and consequently the public money must remain in that institution to the last hour of its existence unless the Secretary of the Treasury shall remove it at an earlier day. The responsibility is thus thrown upon the executive branch of the Government of deciding how long before the expiration of the charter the public interest will require the deposits to be placed elsewhere;. . .And while the President anxiously wishes to abstain from the exercise of doubtful powers and to avoid all interference with the rights and duties of others, he must yet with unshaken constancy discharge his own obligations, and can not allow himself to turn aside in order to avoid any responsibility which the high trust with which he has been honored requires him to encounter; and it being the duty of one of the Executive Departments to decide in the first instance, subject to the future action of the legislative power, whether the public deposits shall remain in the Bank of the United States until the end of its existence or be withdrawn some time before, the President has felt himself bound to examine the question carefully and deliberately in order to make up his judgment on the subject, and in his opinion the near approach of the termination of the charter and the public considerations heretofore mentioned are of themselves amply sufficient to justify the removal of the deposits, without reference to the conduct of the bank or their safety in its keeping.

But in the conduct of the bank may be found other reasons, very imperative in their character, and which require prompt action. Developments have been made from time to time of its faithlessness as a public agent, its misapplication of public funds, its interference in elections, its efforts by the machinery of committees to deprive the Government directors of a full knowledge of its concerns, and, above all, its flagrant misconduct as recently and unexpectedly disclosed in placing all the funds of the bank, including the money of the Government, at the disposition of the president of the bank as means of operating upon public opinion and procuring a new charter, without requiring him to render a voucher for their disbursement. . . .

With these facts before him in an official report from the Government directors, the President would feel that he was not only responsible for all the abuses and corrputions the bank has committed or may commit, but almost an accomplice in a conspiracy against that Government which he has sworn honestly to administer, if he did not take every step within his constitutional and legal power likely to be efficient in putting an end to these enormities. If it be possible within the scope of human affairs to find a reason for removing the Government deposits and leaving the bank to its own resource for the means of effecting its criminal designs, we have it here. Was it expected when the moneys of the United States were directed to be placed in that bank that they would be put under the control of one man empowered to spend millions without rendering a voucher or specifying the object? Can they be considered safe with the evidence before us that tens of thousands have been spent for highly improper, if not corrupt, purposes, and that the same motive may lead to the expenditure of hundreds of thousands, and even millions, more? And can we justify ourselves to the people by longer lending to it the money and power of the Government to be employed for such purposes?

It has been alleged by some as an objection to the removal of the deposits that the bank has the power, and in that event will have the disposition, to destroy the State banks employed by the Government, and bring distress upon the country. It has been the fortune of the President to encounter dangers which were represented as equally alarming, and he has seen them vanish before resolution and energy. Pictures equally appalling were paraded before him when this bank came to demand a new charter. But what was the result? Has the country been ruined, or even distressed? Was it ever more prosperous than since that act? The President verily believes the bank has not the power to produce the calamities its friends threaten. . . . But if the President believed the bank possessed all the power which has been attributed to it, his determination would only be rendered the more inflexible. If, indeed, this corporation now holds in its hands the happiness and prosperity of the American people, it is high time to take the alarm. If the despotism be already upon us and our only safety is in the mercy of the despot, recent developments in relation to his designs and the means he employs show how necessary it is to shake it off. The struggle can never come with less distress to the people or under more favorable auspices than at the present moment.

All doubt as to the willingness of the State banks to undertake the service of the Government to the same extent and on the same terms as it is now performed by the Bank of the United States is put to rest by the report of the agent recently employed to collect information, and from that willingness their own safety in the operation may be confidently inferred. Knowing their own resources better than they can be known by others, it is not to be supposed that they would be willing to place themselves in a situation which they can not occupy without danger of annihilation or embarrassment. The only consideration applies to the safety of the public funds if deposited in .those institutions, and when it is seen that the directors of many of them are not only willing to pledge the character and capital of the corporations in giving success to this measure, but also their own property and reputation, we can not doubt that they at least believe the public deposits would be safe in their management. The President thinks that these facts and circumstances afford as strong a guaranty as can be had in human affairs for the safety of the public funds and the practicability of a new system of collection and disbursement through the agency of the State banks.

From all these considerations the President thinks that the State banks ought immediately to be employed in the collection and disbursement of the public revenue, and the funds now in the Bank of the United States drawn out with all convenient dispatch. . . .The banks to be employed must remit the moneys of the Government without charge, as the Bank of the United States now does; must render all the services which that bank now performs; must keep the Government advised of their situation by periodical returns; in fine, in any arrangement with the State banks the Government must not in any respect be placed on a worse footing than it now is. . . .

As one of the most serious objections to the Bank of the United States is the power which it concentrates, care must be taken in finding other agents for the service of the Treasury not to raise up another power equally formidable. Although it would probably be impossible to produce such a result by any organization of the State banks which could be devised, yet it is desirable to avoid even the appearance. To this end it would be expedient to assume no more power over them and interfere no more in their affairs than might be absolutely necessary to the security of the public deposit and the faithful performance of their duties as agents of the Treasury. . . .

It is the desire of the President that the control of the banks and the currency shall, as far as possible, be entirely separated from the political power of the country as well as wrested from an institution which has already attempted to subject the Government to its will. In his opinion the action of the General Government on this subject ought not to extend beyond the grant in the Constitution, which only authorizes Congress "to coin money and regulate the value thereof;" all else belongs to the States and the people, and must be regulated by public opinion and the interests of trade.

In conclusion, the President must be permitted to remark that he looks upon the pending question as of higher consideration than the mere transfer of a sum of money from one bank to another. Its decision may affect the character of our Government for ages to come. Should the bank be suffered longer to use the public moneys in the accomplishment of its purposes, with the proofs of its faithlessness and corruption before our eyes, the patriotic among our citizens will despair of success in struggling against its power, and we shall be responsible for entailing it upon our country forever. Viewing it as a question of transcendent importance, both in the principles and consequences it involves, the President could not, in justice to the responsibility which he owes to the country, refrain from pressing upon the Secretary of the Treasury his view of the considerations which impel to immediate action. . . .

In the remarks he has made on this all-important question he trusts the Secretary of the Treasury will see only the frank and respectful declarations of the opinions which the President has formed on a measure of great national interest deeply affecting the character and usefulness of his Administration, and not a spirit of dictation, which the President would be as careful to avoid as ready to resist. Happy will he be if the facts now disclosed produce uniformity of opinion and unity of action among the members of the Administration.

The President again repeats that he begs his Cabinet to consider the proposed measure as his own, in the support of which he shall require no one of them to make a sacrifice of opinion or principle. Its responsibility has been assumed after the most mature deliberation and reflection as necessary to preserve the morals of the people, the freedom of the press, and the purity of the elective franchise, without which all will unite in saying that the blood and treasure expended by our forefathers in the establishment of our happy system of government will have been vain and fruitless. Under these convictions he feels that a measure so important to the American people can not be commenced too soon, and he therefore names the 1st day of October next as a period proper for the change of the deposits, or sooner, provided the necessary arrangements with the State banks can be made.

ANDREW JACKSON.

FIFTH ANNUAL MESSAGE
December 3, 1833

*The tariff controversy settled by compromise, Jackson
gave an account in this message of the removal of the
public deposits from the Second Bank of the United
States. However, he omitted reference to the resolutions passed in the Senate censuring his conduct in
these removals.*

Fellow-Citizens of the Senate and the House of Representatives:

On your assembling to perform the high trusts which the people
of the United States have confided to you,. . .it gives me pleasure to
congratulate you upon the happy condition of our beloved country. . . .

Our condition abroad is no less honorable than it is prosperous
at home. Seeking nothing that is not right and determined to submit
to nothing that is wrong, but desiring honest friendships and liberal
intercourse with all nations, the United States have gained throughout
the world the confidence and respect which are due to a policy so
just and so congenial to the character of the American people and to
the spirit of their institutions. . . .

Notwithstanding that I continue to receive the most amicable assur-
ances from the Government of France,. . .it is to be regretted that the
stipulations of the convention concluded on the 4th July, 1831, remain
in some important parts unfulfilled. . . .

Under these circumstances, in a case so important to the interests
of our citizens and to the character of our country, and under dis-
appointments so unexpected, I deemed it my duty. . .no longer to
delay the appointment of a minister plenipotentiary to Paris, but
to dispatch him in season to communicate the result of his application to the French Government at an early period of your session.
I accordingly appointed a distinguished citizen for this purpose, who
proceeded on his mission in August last. . .He is particularly instructed as to all matters connected with the present posture of affairs, and I indulge the hope that. . .the subject will be early considered, and satisfactorily disposed of at the next meeting of the Chambers. . .

It gives me great pleasure to congratulate you upon the prosperous
condition of the finances of the country. . . .

From this view of the state of the finances and the public engagements yet to be fulfilled you will perceive that if Providence permits
me to meet you at another session I shall have the high gratification
of announcing to you that the national debt is extinguished. I can

not refrain from expressing the pleasure I feel at the near approach of that desirable event. The short period of time within which the public debt will have been discharged is strong evidence of the abundant resources of the country and of the prudence and economy with which the Government has heretofore been administered. We have waged two wars since we became a nation, with one of the most powerful kingdoms in the world, both of them undertaken in defense of our dearest rights, both successfully prosecuted and honorably terminated; and many of those who partook in the first struggle as well as in the second will have lived to see the last item of the debt incurred in these necessary but expensive conflicts faithfully and honestly discharged. And we shall have the proud satisfaction of bequeathing to the public servants who follow us in the administration of the Government the rare blessing of a revenue sufficiently abundant, raised without injustice or oppression to our citizens, and unencumbered with any burdens but what they themselves shall think proper to impose upon it. . . .

No more money will afterwards be needed than what may be necessary to meet the ordinary expenses of the Government. Now, then, is the proper moment to fix our system of expenditure on firm and durable principles, and I can not too strongly urge the necessity of a rigid economy and an inflexible determination not to enlarge the income beyond the real necessities of the Government and not to increase the wants of the Government by unnecessary and profuse expenditures. . . .

Since the last adjournment of Congress the Secretary of the Treasury has directed the money of the United States to be deposited in certain State banks designated by him, and he will immediately lay before you his reasons for this direction. I concur with him entirely in the view he has taken of the subject, and some months before the removal I urged upon the Department the propriety of taking that step. The near approach of the day on which the charter will expire, as well as the conduct of the bank, appeared to me to call for this measure upon the high considerations of public interest and public duty. The extent of its misconduct, however, although known to be great, was not at that time fully developed by proof. It was not until late in the month of August that I received from the Government directors an official report establishing beyond question that this great and powerful institution had been actively engaged in attempting to influence the elections of the public officers by means of its money, and that, in violation of the express provisions of its charter, it had by a formal resolution placed its funds at the disposition of its president to be employed in sustaining the political power of the bank. A copy of this resolution is contained in the report of the Government directors before referred to, and however the object may be disguised by cautious language, no one can doubt that this money was in truth intended for electioneering purposes, and the particular uses to which it was proved to have been applied abundantly show that it was so understood. Not only was the evidence complete as to the past application of the money and power of the bank to electioneering purposes, but that the resolution of the board of directors authorized the same course to be pursued in future.

It being thus established by unquestionable proof that the Bank of the United States was converted into a permanent electioneering engine, it appeared to me that the path of duty which the executive department of the Government ought to pursue was not doubtful. As by the terms of the bank charter no officer but the Secretary of the Treasury could remove the deposits, it seemed to me that this authority ought to be at once exerted to deprive that great corporation of the support and countenance of the Government in such an use of its funds and such an exertion of its power. In this point of the case the question is distinctly presented whether the people of the United States are to govern through representatives chosen by their unbiased suffrages or whether the money and power of a great corporation are to be secretly exerted to influence their judgment and control their decisions. . . .

At this time the efforts of the bank to control public opinion, through the distresses of some and the fears of others, are equally apparent, and, if possible, more objectionable. By a curtailment of its accommodations more rapid than any emergency requires, and even while it retains specie to an almost unprecedented amount in its vaults, it is attempting to produce great embarrassment in one portion of the community, while through presses known to have been sustained by its money it attempts by unfounded alarms to create a panic in all.

These are the means by which it seems to expect that it can force a restoration of the deposits, and as a necessary consequence extort from Congress a renewal of its charter. I am happy to know that through the good sense of our people the effort to get up a panic has hitherto failed, and that through the increased accommodations which the State banks have been enabled to afford, no public distress has followed the exertions of the bank, and it can not be doubted that the exercise of its power and the expenditure of its money, as well as its efforts to spread groundless alarm, will be met and rebuked as they deserve. In my own sphere of duty I should feel myself called on by the facts disclosed to order a *scire facias* against the bank, with a view to put an end to the chartered rights it has so palpably violated, were it not that the charter itself will expire as soon as a decision would probably be obtained from the court of last resort. . . .

ANDREW JACKSON.

JACKSON'S PROTEST OF SENATE CENSURE RESOLUTION
April 15, 1834

> *Opposition to the removal of the deposits led to a*
> *Senate request for a copy of the preceding document*
> *in this collection which Jackson had read to his Cabi-.*
> *net. When Jackson refused the request on grounds of*
> *the independence of the executive branch, a Senate*
> *resolution censured the President. Jackson responded*
> *with a "Protest" directed to the Senate but designed*
> *also to win public support. The Senate, however,*
> *refused to enter Jackson's Protest on its journal, and*
> *it was not until January 16, 1837 that the censure*
> *resolution was expunged through the efforts of Thomas*
> *Hart Benton.*

To the Senate of the United States:

It appears by the published Journal of the Senate that on the 26th of December last a resolution was offered by a member of the Senate, which after a protracted debate was on the 28th day of March last modified by the mover and passed by the votes of twenty-six Senators out of forty-six who were present and voted, in the following words,· viz:

"Resolved, That the President, in the late Executive proceedings in relation to the public revenue, has assumed upon himself authority and power not conferred by the Constitution and laws, but in derogation of both."

Having had the honor, through the voluntary suffrages of the American people, to fill the office of President of the United States during the period which may be presumed to have been referred to in this resolution, it is sufficiently evident that the censure it inflicts was intended for myself. Without notice, unheard and untried, I thus find myself charged on the records of the Senate, and in a form hitherto unknown in our history, with the high crime of violating the laws and Constitution of my country. . . .

Bound to the performance of this duty by the oath I have taken, by the strongest obligations of gratitude to the American people, and by the ties which unite my every earthly interest with the welfare and glory of my country, and perfectly convinced that the discussion and passage of the above-mentioned resolution were not only unauthorized by the Constitution, but in many respects repugnant to its provisions and subversive of the rights secured by it to other coordinate departments, I deem it an imperative duty to maintain the supremacy of that sacred instrument and the immunities of the department intrusted to my care by all means consistent with my own lawful powers, with the rights of others, and with the genius of our civil institutions. To this end I have caused this my solemn protest against the aforesaid proceedings to be placed on the files of the executive department and to be transmitted to the Senate. . . .

Under the Constitution of the United States the powers and functions of the various departments of the Federal Government and their responsibilities for violation or neglect of duty are clearly defined or result by necessary inference. . . .

The responsibilities of the President are numerous and weighty. He is liable to impeachment for high crimes and misdemeanors, and on due conviction to removal from office and perpetual disqualification; and notwithstanding such conviction, he may also be indicted and punished according to law. He is also liable to the private action of any party who may have been injured by his illegal mandates or instructions in the same manner and to the same extent as the humblest functionary. In addition to the responsibilities which may thus be enforced by impeachment, criminal prosecution, or suit at law, he is also accountable at the bar of public opinion for every act of his Administration. Subject only to the restraints of truth and justice, the free people of the United States have the undoubted right, as individuals or collectively, orally or in writing, at such times and in such language and form as they may think proper, to discuss his official conduct and to express and promulgate their opinons concerning it. Indirectly also his conduct may come under review in either branch of the Legislature, or in the Senate when acting in its executive capacity, and so far as the executive or legislative proceedings of these bodies may require it, it may be exercised by them. These are believed to be the proper and only modes in which the President of the United States is to be held accountable for his official conduct.

Tested by these principles, the resolution of the Senate is wholly unauthorized by the Constitution, and in derogation of its entire spirit. It assumes that a single branch of the legislative department may for the purposes of a public censure, and without any view to legislation or impeachment, take up, consider, and decide upon the official acts of the Executive. But in no part of the Constitution is the President subjected to any such responsibility, and in no part of that instrument is any such power conferred on either branch of the Legislature. . . .

The President of the United States, therefore, has been by a majority of his constitutional triers accused and found guilty of an impeachable offense, but in no part of this proceeding have the directions of the Constitution been observed.

The impeachment, instead of being preferred and prosecuted by the House of Representatives, originated in the Senate, and was prosecuted without the aid or concurrence of the other House. The oath or affirmation prescribed by the Constitution was not taken by the Senators, the Chief Justice did not preside, no notice of the charge was given to the accused, and no opportunity afforded him to respond to the accusation, to meet his accusers face to face, to cross-examine the witnesses, to procure counteracting testimony, or to be heard in his defense. The safeguards and formalities which the Constitution has connected with the power of impeachment were doubtless supposed by the framers of that instrument to be essential to the protection of the public servant, to the attainment of justice, and to the order, impartiality, and dignity of the procedure. These safeguards and formalities were not only practically disregarded in the commencement and conduct of these proceedings, but in their result I find myself convicted by less than two-thirds of the members present of an impeachable offense.

In vain may it be alleged in defense of this proceeding that the form of the resolution is not that of an impeachment. . .It is because it did not assume the form of an impeachment that it is the more palpably repugnant to the Constitution, for it is through that form only that the President is judicially responsible to the Senate;. . .

Nearly forty-five years had the President exercised, without a question to his rightful authority, those powers for the recent assumption of which he is now denounced. The vicissitudes of peace and war had attended our Government; violent parties, watchful to take advantage of any seeming usurption on the part of the Executive, had distracted our councils; frequent removals, or forced resignations in every sense tantamount to removals, had been made of the Secretary and other officers of the Treasury, and yet in no one instance is it known that any man, whether patriot or partisan, had raised his voice against it as a violation of the Constitution. The expediency and justice of such changes in reference to public officers of all grades have frequently been the topic of discussion, but the consitutional right of the President to appoint, control, and remove the head of the Treasury as well as all other Departments seems to have been universally conceded. And what is the occasion upon which other principles have been first officially asserted? The Bank of the United States, a great moneyed monopoly, had attempted to obtain a renewal of its charter by controlling the elections of the people and the action of the Government. The use of its corporate funds and power in that attempt was fully disclosed, and it was made known to the President that the corporation was putting in train the same course of measures, with the view of making another vigorous effort, through an interference in the elections of the people, to control public opinion and force the Government to yield to its demands. This, with its corruption of the press, its violation of its charter, its exclusion of the Government directors from its proceedings, its neglect of duty and arrogant pretensions, made it, in the opinion of the President, incompatible with the public interest and the safety of our institutions that it should be longer employed as the fiscal agent of the Treasury. . . .

The dangerous tendency of the doctrine which denies to the President the power of supervising, directing, and controlling the Secretary of the Treasury in like manner with the other executive officers would soon be manifest in practice were the doctrine to be established. The President is the direct representative of the American people, but the Secretaries are not. If the Secretary of the Treasury be independent of the President in the execution of the laws, then is there no direct responsibility to the people in that important branch of this Government to which is committed the care of the national finances. And it is in the power of the Bank of the United States, or any other corporation, body of men, or individuals, if a Secretary shall be found to accord with them in opinion or can be induced in practice to promote their views, to control through him the whole action of the Government (so far as it is exercised by his Department) in defiance of the Chief Magistrate elected by the people and responsible to them.

But the evil tendency of the particular doctrine adverted to, though sufficiently serious, would be as nothing in comparison with the pernicious consequences which would inevitably flow from the approbation and allowance by the people and the practice by the Senate of the unconstitutional power of arraigning and censuring the official conduct of the Executive in the manner recently pursued. Such proceedings are eminently calculated to unsettle the foundations of the Government, to disturb the harmonious action of its different departments, and to break down the checks and balances by which the wisdom of its framers sought to insure its stability and usefulness. . . .

The influence of such proceedings on the other departments of the Government, and more especially on the States, could not fail to be extensively pernicious. When the judges in the last resort of official misconduct themselves overlap the bounds of their authority as prescribed by the Constitution, what general disregard of its provisions might not their example be expected to produce? And who does not perceive that such contempt of the Federal Constitution by one of its most important departments would hold out the strongest temptations to resistance on the part of the State sovereignties whenever they shall suppose their just rights to have been invaded?. . .

Far be it from me to charge or to insinuate that the present Senate of the United States intend in the most distant way to encourage such a result. It is not of their motives or designs, but only of the tendency of their acts, that it is my duty to speak. . . .It is due to the high trust with which I have been charged, to those who may be called to succeed me in it, to the representatives of the people whose constitutional prerogative has been unlawfully assumed, to the people and to the States, and to the Constitution they have established that I should not permit its provisions to be broken down by such an attack on the executive department without at least some effort "to preserve, protect, and defend" them. With this view, and for the reasons which have been stated, I do hereby solemnly protest against the aforementioned proceedings of the Senate as unauthorized by the Constitution, contrary to its spirit and to several of its express provisions, subversive of that distribution of the powers of government which it has ordained and established, destructive of the checks and safeguards by which these powers were intended on the one hand to be controlled and on the other to be protected, and calculated by their immediate and collateral effects, by their character and tendency, to concentrate in the hands of a body not directly amenable to the people a degree of influence and power dangerous to their liberties and fatal to the Constitution of their choice.

The resolution of the Senate contains an imputation upon my private as well as upon my public character, and as it must stand forever on their journals, I can not close this substitute for that defense which I have not been allowed to present in the ordinary form without remarking that I have lived in vain if it be necessary to enter into a formal vindication of my character and purposes from such an imputation. In vain do I bear upon my person enduring memorials of that contest in which American liberty was purchased; in vain have I since periled property, fame, and life in defense of the rights and privileges so dearly bought; in vain am I now, without a personal aspiration or the hope of individual advantage, encountering responsibilities and dangers from which by mere inactivity in relation to a single point I might have been exempt, if any serious doubts can be entertained as to the purity of my purposes and motives. If I had been ambitious, I should have sought an alliance with that powerful institution which even now aspires to no divided empire. If I had been venal, I should have sold myself to its designs. Had

I preferred personal comfort and official ease to the performance of my arduous duty, I should have ceased to molest it. In the history of conquerors and usurpers, never in the fire of youth nor in the vigor of manhood could I find an attraction to lure me from the path of duty, and now I shall scarcely find an inducement to commence their career of ambition when gray hairs and a decaying frame, instead of inviting to toil and battle, call me to the contemplation of other worlds, where conquerors cease to be honored and usurpers expiate their crimes. The only ambition I can feel is to acquit myself to Him to whom I must soon render an account of my stewardship, to serve my fellowmen, and live respected and honored in the history of my country. No; the ambition which leads me on is an anxious desire and a fixed determination to return to the people unimpaired the sacred trust they have confided to my charge; to heal the wounds of the Constitution and preserve it from further violation; to persuade my countrymen, so far as I may, that it is not in a splendid government supported by powerful monopolies and aristocratical establishments that they will find happiness or their liberties protection, but in a plain system, void of pomp, protecting all and granting favors to none, dispensing its blessings, like the dews of Heaven, unseen and unfelt save in the freshness and beauty they contribute to produce. It is such a government that the genius of our people requires; such an one only under which our States may remain for ages to come united, prosperous, and free. If the Almighty Being who has hitherto sustained and protected me will but vouchsafe to make my feeble power, instrumental to such a result, I shall anticipate with pleasure the place to be assigned me in the history of my country, and die contented with the belief that I have contributed in some small degree to increase the value and prolong the duration of American liberty.

To the end that the resolution of the Senate may not be hereafter drawn into precedent with the authority of silent acquiescence on the part of the executive department, and to the end also that my motives and views in the Executive proceedings denounced in that resolution may be known to my fellow-citizens, to the world, and to all posterity, I respectfully request that this message and protest may be entered at length of the journals of the Senate.

ANDREW JACKSON.

April 21, 1834

To the Senate of the United States:

Having reason to believe that certain passages contained in my message and protest transmitted to the Senate on the 17th [15th] instant may be misunderstood, I think it proper to state that it was not my intention to deny in the said message the power and right of the legislative department to provide by law for the custody, safe-keeping, and disposition of the public money and property of the United States. . . .

I admit without reserve, as I have before done, the constitutional power of the Legislature to prescribe by law the place or places in which the public money or other property is to be desposited, and to make such regulations concerning its custody, removal, or disposition as they may think proper to enact. Nor do I claim for the Executive any right to the possession or disposition of the public property or treasure or any authority to interfere with the same, except when such possession, disposition, or authority is given to him by law. Nor do I claim the right in any manner to supervise or interfere with the person intrusted with such property or treasure, unless he be an officer whose appointment, under the Constitution and laws, is devolved upon the President alone or in conjunction with the Senate, and for whose conduct he is constitutionally responsible. . . .

I have therefore respectfully to request that this communication may be considered a part of that message and that it may be entered therewith on the journals of the Senate.

ANDREW JACKSON.

SIXTH ANNUAL MESSAGE
December 1, 1834

Angered by the prolonged refusal of the French to make payment on the 25,000,000 francs in spoliation claims agreed to in 1832, Jackson recommended to Congress the enactment of a law authorizing reprisals. He again proscribed the national bank and summarized his position on internal improvements, closing with a carefully qualified wish that the latter might be extended to every part of the country.

Fellow-Citizens of the Senate and House of Representatives:

In performing my duty at the opening of your present session it gives me pleasure to congratulate you again upon the prosperous condition of our beloved country. . . .

The history of the accumulated and unprovoked aggressions upon our commerce committed by authority of the existing Governments of France between the years 1800 and 1817 has been rendered too painfully familiar to Americans to make its repetition either necessary or desirable. . . .After the most deliberate and thorough examination of the whole subject a treaty between the two Governments was concluded and signed at Paris on the 4th of July, 1831, by which it was stipulated that "the French Government, in order to liberate itself from all the reclamations preferred against it by citizens of the United States for unlawful seizures, captures, sequestrations, confiscations, or destruction of their vessels, cargoes, or other property, engages to pay a sum of 25,000,000 francs to the United States, who shall distribute it among those entitled in the manner and according to the rules it shall determine;" and it was also stipulated on the part of the French Government that this 25,000,000 francs should "be paid at Paris, in six annual installments of 4,166,666 francs and 66 centimes each, into the hands of such person or persons as shall be authorized by the Government of the United States to receive it," the first installment to be paid "at the expiration of one year next following the exchange of the ratifications of this convention and the others at successive intervals of a year, one after another, till the whole shall be paid. To the amount of each of the said installments shall be added interest at 4 per cent thereupon, as upon the other installments then remaining unpaid, the said interest to be computed from the day of the exchange of the present convention."

It was also stipulated on the part of the United States, for the purpose of being completely liberated from all the reclamations presented by France on behalf of its citizens, that the sum of 1,500,000 francs should be paid to the Government of France in six annual installments. . . . .

This treaty was duly ratified in the manner prescribed by the constitutions of both countries, and the ratification was exchanged at the city of Washington on the 2d of Feburary, 1832. . . .The faith of the French nation having been thus solemnly pledged through its consittutional organ for the liquidation and ultimate payment of the long-deferred claims of our citizens, as also for the adjustment of other points of great and reciprocal benefits to both countries, and the United States having. . . done everything that was necessary to carry the treaty into full and fair effect on their part, counted with the most perfect confidence on equal fidelity and promptitude on the part of the French Government. In this reasonable expectation we have been, I regret to inform you, wholly disappointed. No legislative provision has been made by France for the execution of the treaty, either as it respects the indemnity to be paid or the commercial benefits to be secured to the United States, and the relations between the United States and that power in consequence thereof are placed in a situation threatening to interrupt the good understanding which has so long and so happily existed between the two nations. ·

Not only has the French Government been thus wanting in the performance of the stipulations it has so solemnly entered into with the United States, but its omissions have been marked by circumstances which would seem to leave us without satisfactory evidences that such performance will certainly take place at a future period. . . .

It is my conviction that the United States ought to insist on a prompt execution of the treaty, and in case it be refused or longer delayed take redress into their own hands. After the delay on the part of France of a quarter of a century in acknowledging these claims by treaty, it is not to be tolerated that another quarter of a century is to be wasted in negotiating about the payment. The laws of nations provide a remedy for such occasions. It is a well-settled principle of the international code that where one nation owes another a liquidated debt which it refuses or neglects to pay the aggrieved party may seize on the property belonging to the other, its citizens or subjects, sufficient to pay the debt without giving just cause of war. . . .

Since France, in violation of the pledges given through her minister here, has delayed her final action so long that her decision will not probably be known in time to be communicated to this Congress, I recommend that a law be passed authorizing reprisals upon French property in case provision shall not be made for the payment of the debt at the approaching session of the French Chambers. Such a measure ought not to be considered by France as a menace. Her pride and power are too well known to expect anything from her fears and preclude the necessity of a declaration that nothing partaking of the character of intimidation is intended by us. She ought to look upon it as the evidence only of an inflexible determination on the part of the United States to insist on their rights. The Government, by doing only what it has itself acknowledged to be just, will be able to spare the United States the necessity of taking redress into their own hands and save the property of French citizens from that seizure and sequestration which American citizens so long endured without retaliation or redress. If she should continue to refuse that act of acknowledged justice and, in violation of the law of nations, make reprisals on our part the occasion of hostilities against the United States, she would but add violence to injustice, and could not fail to expose herself to the just censure of civilized nations and to the retributive judgments of Heaven.

Collision with France is the more to be regretted on account of the position she occupies in Europe in relation to liberal institutions, but in maintaining our national rights and honor all governments are alike to us. If by a collision with France in a case where she is clearly in the wrong the march of liberal principles shall be impeded, the responsibility for that result as well as every other will rest on her own head.

Having submitted these considerations, it belongs to Congress to decide whether after what has taken place it will still await the further action of the French Chambers or now adopt such provisional measures as it may deem necessary and best adapted to protect the rights and maintain the honor of the country. . . .

Circumstances make it my duty to call the attention of Congress to the Bank of the United States. Created for the convenience of the Government, that institution has become the scourge of the people. Its interference to postpone the payment of a portion of the national debt that it might retain the public money appropriated for that purpose to strengthen it in a political contest, the extraordinary extension and contraction of its accommodations to the community, its corrupt and partisan loans, its exclusion of the public directors from a knowledge of its most important proceedings, the unlimited authority conferred on the president to expend its funds in hiring writers and procuring the execution of printing, and the use made of that authority, the retention of the pension money and books after the selection of new agents, the groundless claim to heavy damages in consequence of the protest of the bill drawn on the French Government, have through various channels been laid before Congress. . . .

It seems due to the safety of the public funds remaining in that bank and to the honor of the American people that measures be taken to separate the Government entirely from an institution so michievous to the public prosperity and so regardless of the Constitution and laws. By transferring the public deposits, by appointing other pension agents as far as it had the power, by ordering the discontinuance of the receipt of bank checks in the payment of the public dues after the 1st day of January, the Executive has exerted all its lawful authority to sever the connection between the Government and this faithless corporation.

The high-handed career of this institution imposes upon the constitutional functionaries of this Government duties of the gravest and most imperative character—duties which they can not avoid and from which I trust there will be no inclination on the part of any of them to shrink. My own sense of them is most clear, as is also my readiness to discharge those which may rightfully fall on me. To continue any business relations with the Bank of the United States that may be avoided without a violation of the national faith after that institution has set at open defiance the conceded right of the Government to examine its affairs, after it has done all in its power to deride the public authority in other respects and to bring it into disrepute at home and abroad, after it has attempted to defeat the clearly expressed will of the people by turning against them the immense power intrusted to its hands and by involving a country otherwise peaceful, flourishing, and happy, in dissension, embarrassment, and distress, would make the nation itself a party to the degradation so sedulously prepared for its public agents and do much to destroy the confidence of mankind in popular governments and to bring into contempt their authority and efficiency. In guarding against an evil of such magnitude considerations of temporary convenience should be thrown out of the question, and we should be influenced by such motives only as look to the honor and preservation of the republican system. Deeply and solemnly impressed with the justice of these views, I feel it to be my duty to recommend to you that a law be passed authorizing the sale of the public stock; that the provision of the charter requiring the receipt of notes of the bank in payment of public dues shall, in accordance with the power reserved to Congress in the fourteenth section of the charter, be suspended until the bank pays to the Treasury the dividends withheld, and that all laws connecting the Government or its officers with the bank, directly or indirectly, be repealed, and that the institution be left hereafter to its own resources and means.

Events have satisfied my mind, and I think the minds of the American people, that the mischiefs and dangers which flow from a national bank far overbalance all its advantages. The bold effort the present bank has made to control the Government, the distresses it has wantonly produced, the violence of which it has been the occasion in one of our citites famed for its observance of law and order, are but premonitions of the fate which awaits the American people should they be deluded into a perpetuation of this institution or the establishment of another like it. . . .

Happily it is already illustrated that the agency of such an institution is not necessary to the fiscal operations of the Government. The State banks are found fully adequate to the performance of all services which were required of the Bank of the United States, quite as promptly and with the same cheapness. They have maintained themselves and discharged all these duties while the Bank of the United States was still powerful and in the field as an open enemy, and it is not possible to conceive that they will find greater difficulties in their operations when that enemy shall cease to exist. . . .

There can be no question connected with the administration of public affairs more important or more difficult to be satisfactorily dealt with than that which relates to the rightful authority and proper action of the Federal Government upon the subject of internal improvements. . . .

The questions which have arisen upon this subject have related—

First. To the power of making internal improvements within the limits of a State, with the right of territorial jurisdiction, sufficient at least for their preservation and use.

Second. To the right of appropriating money in aid of such works when carried on by a State or by a company in virtue of State authority, surrendering the claim of jurisdiction; and

Third. To the propriety of appropriation for improvements of a particular class, viz, for light-houses, beacons, buoys, public piers, and for the removal of sand bars, sawyers, and other temporary and partial impediments in our navigable rivers and harbors.

The claims of power for the General Government upon each of these points certainly present matter of the deepest interest. The first is, however, of much the greatest importance, inasmuch as, in addition to the dangers of unequal and improvident expenditures of public moneys common to all, there is superadded to that the conflicting jurisdictions of the respective governments. . . .The powers exercised by the Federal Government would soon be regarded with jealousy by the State authorities, and originating as they must from implication or assumption, it would be impossible to affix to them certain and safe limits. Opportunities and temptations to the assumption of power incompatible with State sovereignty would be increased and those barriers which resist the tendency of our system toward consolidation greatly weakened. . . .

Regarding the bill authorizing a subscription to the stock of the Maysville and Lexington Turnpike Company as the entering wedge of a system which, however weak at first, might soon become strong enough to rive the bands of the Union asunder, and believing that if its passage was acquiesced in by the Executive and the people there would no longer be any limitation upon the authority of the General Government in respect to the appropriation of money for such objects, I deemed it an imperative duty to withhold from it the Executive approval. Although from the obviously local character of that work I might well have contented myself with a refusal to approve the bill upon that ground, yet sensible of the vital importance of the subject, and anxious that my views and opinions in regard to the whole matter should be fully understood by Congress and by my constituents, I felt it my duty to go further. I therefore embraced that early occasion to apprise Congress that in my opinion the Constitution did not confer upon it the power to authorize the construction of ordinary roads and canals within the limits of a State and to say, respectfully, that no bill admitting such a power could receive my official sanction. . . .

So far, at least, as it regards this branch of the subject, my best hopes have been realized. Nearly four years have elapsed, and several sessions of Congress have intervened, and no attempt within my recollection has been made to induce Congress to exercise this power. The applications for the construction of roads and canals which were formerly multiplied upon your files are no longer presented, and we have good reason to infer that the current of public sentiment has become so decided against the pretension as effectually to discourage its reassertion. So thinking, I derive the greatest satisfaction from the conviction that thus much at least has been secured upon this important and embarrassing subject.

From attempts to appropriate the national funds to objects which are confessedly of a local character we can not, I trust, have anything further to apprehend. My views in regard to the expediency of making appropriations for works which are claimed to be of a national character and prosecuted under State authority—assuming that Congress have the right to do so—were stated in my annual message to Congress in 1830, and also in that containing my objections to the Maysville road bill. . . .

There is another class of appropriations for what may be called, without impropriety, internal improvements, which have always been regarded as standing upon different grounds from those to which I have referred. I allude to such as have for their object the improvement of our harbors, the removal of partial and temporary obstructions in our navigable rivers, for the facility and security of our foreign commerce. . . . The convenience and safety of this commerce have led to the gradual extension of these expenditures; to the erection of light-houses, the placing, planting, and sinking of buoys, beacons, and piers and to the removal of partial and temporary obstruction in our navigable rivers and in the harbors upon our Great Lakes as well as on the seaboard. Although I have expressed to Congress my apprehension that these expenditures have sometimes been extravagant and disproportionate to the advantages to be derived from them, I have not felt it to be my duty to refuse my assent to bills containing them, and have contented myself to follow in this respect in the footsteps of all my predecessors. . . .

I am not hostile to internal improvements, and wish to see them extended to every part of the country. But I am fully persuaded, if they are not commenced in a proper manner, confined to proper objects, and conducted under an authority generally conceded to be rightful, that a successful prosecution of them can not be reasonably expected. The attempt will meet with resistance where it might otherwise receive support, and instead of strengthening the bonds of our Confederacy it will only multiply and aggravate the causes of disunion.

ANDREW JACKSON.

SEVENTH ANNUAL MESSAGE
December 7, 1835

Jackson used this message to diplomatic effect as he continued to press for settlement of the French Spoliation claims. His denial of "menace or insult" to France in his previous message to Congress satisfied the French desire for explanation and the debt was paid by 1836. At home, Jackson warned again against the "spirit of monopoly" represented by the bank, noted the consummation of his Indian policy, and attacked the use of the mails for sending abolitionist literature into the South.

Fellow-Citizens of the Senate and House of Representatives:

You are assembled at a period of profound interest to the American patriot. The unexampled growth and prosperity of our country having given us a rank in the scale of nations which removes all apprehension of danger to our integrity and independence from external foes, the career of freedom is before us, with an earnest from the past that if true to ourselves there can be no formidable obstacle in the future to its peaceful and uninterrupted pursuit. . . .

We have but to look at the state of our agriculture, manufactures, and commerce and the unexampled increase of our population to feel the magnitude of the trust committed to us. Never in any former period of our history have we had greater reason than we now have to be thankful to Divine Providence for the blessings of health and general prosperity. Every branch of labor we see crowned with the most abundant rewards. In every element of national resources and wealth and of individual comfort we witness the most rapid and solid improvements. . . .

Since the last session of Congress the validity of our claims upon France, as liquidated by the treaty of 1831, has been acknowledged by both branches of her legislature, and the money has been appropriated for their discharge; but the payment is, I regret to inform you, still withheld. . . .

. . . .disappointed in our just expectations, it became my imperative duty to consult with Congress in regard to the expediency of a resort to retaliatory measures in case the stipulations of the treaty should not be speedily complied with, and to recommend such as in my judgment the occasion called for. To this end an unreserved communication of the case in all its aspects became indispensable. . . .
Admonished by the past of the difficulty of making even the simplest

statement of our wrongs without disturbing the sensibilities of those
who had by their position become responsible for their redress, and
earnestly desirous of preventing further obstacles from that source,
I went out of my way to preclude a construction, of the message
by which the recommendation that was made to Congress might
be regarded as a menace to France in not only disavowing such a
design, but in declaring that her pride and her power were too well
known to expect anything from her fears. . . .

Although the message was not officially communicated to the French
Government, and notwithstanding the declaration to the contrary
which it contained, the French ministry decided to consider the conditional recommendation of reprisals a menace and an insult which
the honor of the nation made it incumbent on them to resent. The
measures resorted to by them to evince their sense of the supposed
indignity were the immediate recall of their minister at Washington,
the offer of passports to the American minister at Paris, and a public
notice to the legislative Chambers that all diplomatic intercourse
with the United States had been suspended. . . .

The minister of finance. . .as the organ of the ministry declared
the message, so long as it had not received the sanction of Congress,
a mere expression of the personal opinion of the President, for which
neither the Government nor people of the United States were responsible, and that an engagement had been entered into for the ful-
fillment of which the honor of France was pledged. Entertaining
these views, the single condition which the French ministry proposed
to annex to the payment of the money was that it should not be
made until it was ascertained that the Government of the United
States had done nothing to injure the interests of France, or, in other
words, that no steps had been authorized by Congress of a hostile
character toward France. . . .

The conception that it was my intention to menace or insult the
Government of France is as unfounded as the attempt to extort from
the fears of that nation what her sense of justice may deny would be
vain and ridiculous. . . . The principle which calls in question the
President for the language of his message would equally justify a
foreign power in demanding explanation of the language used in the
report of a committee or by a member in debate. . . .

Not having received any official information of the intentions of
the French Government, and anxious to bring, as far as practicable,
this unpleasant affair to a close before the meeting of Congress, that
you might have the whole subject before you, I caused our charge
d'affaires at Paris to be instructed to ask for the final determination
of the French Government, and in the event of their refusal to pay

the installments now due, without further explanations to return to the United States.

The result of this last application has not yet reached us, but is daily expected. . . .

The honor of my country shall never be stained by an apology from me for the statement of truth and the performance of duty; nor can I give any explanation of my official acts except such as' is due to integrity and justice and consistent with the principles on which our institutions have been framed. This determination will, I am confident, be approved by my constituents. I have, indeed, studied their character to but little purpose if the sum of 25,000,000 francs will have the weight of a feather in the estimation of what appertains to their national independence, and if, unhappily, a different impression should at any time obtain in any quarter, they will, I am sure, rally round the Government of their choice with alacrity and unanimity, and silence forever the degrading imputation. . . .

Since my last annual communication all the remains of the public debt have been redeemed, or money has been placed in deposit for this purpose whenever the creditors choose to receive it. . . .

After the extensive embarrassment and distress recently produced by the Bank of the United States,. . .every candid and intelligent individual must admit that for the attainment of the great advantages of a sound currency we must look to a course of legislation radically different from that which created such an institution. . . .

On this subject I am sure that I can not be mistaken in ascribing our want of success to the undue countenance which has been afforded to the spirit of monopoly. All the serious dangers which our system has yet encountered may be traced to the resort to implied powers and the use of corporations clothed with privileges, the effect of which is to advance the interests of the few at the expense of the many. We have felt but one class of these dangers exhibited in the contest waged by the Bank of the United States against the Government for the last four years. Happily they have been obviated for the present by the indignant resistance of the people, but we should recollect that the principle whence they sprung is an ever-active one, which will not fail to renew its efforts in the same and in other forms so long as there is a hope of success. . . .

We are now to see whether, in the present favorable condition of the country, we can not take an effectual stand against this spirit of monopoly, and practically prove in respect to the currency as well as other important interests that there is no necessity for so extensive a resort to it as that which has been heretofore practiced. The experience of another year has confirmed the utter fallacy of the idea that the Bank of the United States was necessary as a fiscal agent of the Government. Without its aid as such, indeed, in despite of all the embarrassment it was in its power to create, the revenue has been paid with punctuality by our citizens, the business of exchange, both foreign and domestic, has been conducted with convenience, and the circulating medium has been greatly improved. By the use of the State banks, which do not derive their charters from the General Government and are not controlled by its authority, it is ascertained that the moneys of the United States can be collected and disbursed without loss or inconvenience, and that all the wants of the community in relation to exchange and currency are supplied as well as they have ever been before. . . .

Although clothed with the legal authority and supported by precedent, I was aware that there was in the act of the removal of the deposits a liability to excite that sensitiveness to Executive power which it is the characteristic and the duty of freemen to indulge; but I relied on this feeling also, directed by patriotism and intelligence, to vindicate the conduct which in the end would appear to have been called for by the best interests of my country. . . .The result has shewn how safe is this reliance upon the patriotic temper and enlightened discernment of the people. That measure has now been before them and has stood the test of all the severe analysis which its general importance, the interests it affected, and the apprehensions it excited were calculated to produce, and it now remains for Congress to consider what legislation has become necessary in consequence. . . .

The plan of removing the aboriginal people who yet remain within the settled portions of the United States to the country west of the Mississippi River approaches its consummation. . . .Many have already removed and others are preparing to go, and with the exception of two small bands living in Ohio and Indiana, not exceeding 1,500 persons, and of the Cherokees, all the tribes on the east side of the Mississippi, and extending from Lake Michigan to Florida, have entered into engagements which will lead to their transplantation.

The plan for their removal and reestablishment is founded upon the knowledge we have gained of their character and habits, and has been dictated by a spirit of enlarged liberality. A territory exceeding in extent that relinquished has been granted to each tribe. Of its climate, fertility, and capacity to support an Indian population the representations are highly favorable. To these districts the Indians are removed at the expense of the United States, and with certain supplies of clothing, arms, ammunition, and other indispensable articles; they are also furnished gratuitously with provisions for the period of a year after their arrival at their new homes. . . .Ample arrangements have also been made for the support of schools; in some instances council houses and churches are to be erected, dwellings constructed for the chiefs, and mills for common use. Funds have been set apart for the maintenance of the poor; the most necessary mechanical arts have been introduced, and blacksmiths, gunsmiths, wheelwrights, mill-wrights, etc., are supported among them. Steel and iron, and sometimes salt, are purchased for them, and plows and other farming utensils, domestic animals, looms, spinning wheels, cards, etc., are presented to them. And besides these beneficial arrangements, annuities are in all cases paid, amounting in some instances to more than $30 for each individual of the tribe, and in all cases sufficiently great, if justly divided and prudently expended, to enable them, in addition to their own exertions, to live comfortably. . . .

Some general legislation seems necessary for the regulation of the relations which will exist in this new state of things between the Government and people of the United States and these transplanted Indian tribes, and for the establishment among the latter, and with their own consent, of some principles of intercommunication which their juxtaposition will call for; that moral may be substituted for physical force, the authority of a few and simple laws for the tomahawk, and that an end may be put to those bloody wars whose prosecution seems to have made part of their social system.

After the further details of this arrangement are completed, with a very general supervision over them, they ought to be left to the progress of events. These, I indulge the hope, will secure their prosperity and improvement, and a large portion of the moral debt we owe them will then be paid. . . .

In connection with these provisions in relation to the Post-Office Department, I must also invite your attention to the painful excitement produced in the South by attempts to circulate through the mails inflammatory appeals addressed to the passions of the slaves, in prints and in various sorts of publications, calculated to stimulate them to insurrection and to produce all the horrors of a servile war. There is doubtless no respectable portion of our countrymen who can be so far misled as to feel any other sentiment than that of indignant regret at conduct so destructive of the harmony and peace of the country, and so repugnant to the principles of our national compact and to the dictates of humanity and religion. Our happiness and prosperity essentially depend upon peace within our borders, and peace depends upon the maintenance in good faith of those compromises of the Constitution upon which the Union is founded. It is fortunate for the country that the good sense, the generous feeling, and the deep-rooted attachement of the people of the nonslaveholding States to the Union and to their fellow-citizens of the same blood in the South have given so strong and impressive a tone to the sentiments entertained against the proceedings of the misguided persons who have engaged in these unconstitutional and wicked attempts, and especially against the emissaries from foreign parts who have dared to interfere in this matter, as to authorize the hope that those attempts will no longer be persisted in. But if these expressions of the public will shall not be sufficient to effect so desirable a result, not a doubt can be entertained that the nonslaveholding States, so far from countenancing the slightest interference with the constitutional rights of the South, will be prompt to exercise their authority in suppressing so far as in them lies whatever is calculated to produce this evil. . . .

I would therefore call the special attention of Congress to the subject, and respectfully suggest the propriety of passing such a law as will prohibit, under severe penalties, the circulation in the Southern States, through the mail, of incendiary publications intended to instigate the slaves to insurrection.

I felt it to be my duty in the first message which I communicated to Congress to urge upon its attention the propriety of amending that part of the Constitution which provides for the election of the President and the Vice-President of the United States. The leading object which I had in view was the adoption of some new provisions which would secure to the people the performance of this high duty without any intermediate agency. . . .

Considering the great extent of our Confederacy, the rapid increase of its population, and the diversity of their interests and pursuits, it can not be disguised that the contingency by which one branch of the Legislature is to form itself into an electoral college can not become one of ordinary occurrence without producing incalcuable mischief. What was intended as the medicine of the Constitution in extreme cases can not be frequently used without changing its character and sooner or later producing incurable disorder. . . .

ANDREW JACKSON.

EIGHTH ANNUAL MESSAGE
December 5, 1836

In his last annual message Jackson noted the resumption of diplomatic relations with France but introduced a new issue in American foreign affairs, the independence of Texas. At the end of his administrations as at the beginning, financial questions were paramount. He now opposed a constitutional amendment to allow distribution of surplus revenue to the states and reported on the order for the Specie Circular which checked speculation but could not avert the depression of 1837.

Fellow-Citizens of the Senate and House of Representatives:

Addressing to you the last annual message I shall ever present to the Congress of the United States, it is a source of the most heartfelt satisfaction to be able to congratulate you on the high state of prosperity which our beloved country has attained. . . .

With France our diplomatic relations have been resumed, and under circumstances which attest the disposition of both Governments to preserve a mutually beneficial intercourse and foster those amicable feelings which are so strongly required by the true interests of the two countries. . . .

The known desire of the Texans to become a part of our system, although its gratification depends upon the reconcilement of various and conflicting interests, necessarily a work of time and uncertain in itself, is calculated to expose our conduct to misconstruction in the eyes of the world. There are already those who, indifferent to principle themselves and prone to suspect the want of it in others, charge us with ambitious designs and insidious policy. . . .

The experience of other nations admonished us to hasten the extinguishment of the public debt; but it will be in vain that we have congratulated each other upon the disappearance of this evil if we do not guard against the equally great one of promoting the unnecessay accumulation of public revenue. . . .

Under our present revenue system there is every probability that there will continue to be a surplus beyond the wants of the Government, and it has become our duty to decide whether such a result be consistent with the true objects of our Government.

Should a surplus be permitted to accumulate beyond the appropriations, it must be retained in the Treasury, as it now is, or distributed among the people or the States.

To retain it in the Treasury unemployed in any way is impracticable; it is, besides, against the genius of our free institutions to lock up in vaults the treasure of the nation. To take from the people the right of bearing arms and put their weapons of defense in the hands of a standing army would be scarcely more dangerous to their liberties than to permit the Government to accumulate immense amounts of treasure beyond the supplies necessary to its legitimate wants. Such a treasure would doubtless be employed at some time, as it has been in other countries, when opportunity tempted ambition.

To collect it merely for distribution to the States would seem to be highly impolitic, if not as dangerous as the proposition to retain it in the Treasury. . . .

The safest and simplest mode of obviating all the difficulties which have been mentioned is to collect only revenue enough to meet the wants of the Government, and let the people keep the balance of their property in their own hands, to be used for their own profit. . . .

Without desiring to conceal that the experience and observation of the last two years have operated a partial change in my views upon this interesting subject, it is nevertheless regretted that the suggestions made by me in my annual messages of 1829 and 1830 have been greatly misunderstood. At that time the great struggle was begun against that latitudinarian construction of the Constitution which authorizes the unlimited appropriation of the revenues of the Union to internal improvements within the States, tending to invest in the hands and place under the control of the General Government all the principal roads and canals of the country, in violation of State rights and in derogation of State authority. At the same time the condition of the manufacturing interest was such as to create an apprehension that the duties on imports could not without extensive mischief be reduced in season to prevent the accumulation of a considerable surplus after the payment of the national debt. In view of the dangers of such a surplus, and in preference to its application to internal improvements in derogation of the rights and powers of the States, the suggestion of an amendment of the Constitution to authorize its distribution was made. It was an alternative for what were deemed greater evils—a temporary resort to relieve an overburdened treasury until the Government could, without a sudden and destructive revulsion in the business of the country, gradually return to the just principle of raising no more revenue from the people in taxes than is necessary for its economical support. . . . As already intimated, my views have undergone a change so far as to be convinced that no alteration of the Constitution in this respect is wise or expedient. The influence of an accumulating surplus upon the legislation of the General Government and the States, its effect upon the credit system of the country, producing dangerous extensions and ruinous contractions, fluctuations in the price of property, rash speculation, idleness, extravagance, and a deterioration of morals, have taught us the important lesson that any transient mischief which may attend the reduction of our revenue to the wants of our Government is to be borne in preference to an overflowing treasury.

I beg leave to call your attention to another subject intimately associated with the preceding one—the currency of the country. . . .

Variableness must ever be the characteristic of a currency of which the precious metals are not the chief ingredient, or which can be expanded or contracted without regard to the principles that regulate the value of those metals as a standard in the general trade of the world. With us bank issues constitute such a currency, and must ever do so until they are made dependent on those just proportions of gold and silver as a circulating medium which experience has proved to be necessary not only in this but in all other commercial countries. Where those proportions are not infused into the circulation and do not control it, it is manifest that prices must vary according to the tide of bank issues. . . .

In the acts of several of the States prohibiting the circulation of small notes, and the auxiliary enactments of Congress at the last session forbidding their reception or payment on public account, the true policy of the country has been advanced and a larger portion of the precious metals infused into our circulating medium. These measures will probably be followed up in due time by the enactment of State laws banishing from circulation bank notes of still higher denominations, and the object may be materially promoted by further acts of Congress forbidding the employment as fiscal agents of such banks as continue to issue notes of low denominations and throw impediments in the way of the circulation of gold and silver.

The effects of an extension of bank credits and overissues of bank paper have been strikingly illustrated in the sales of the public lands. From the returns made by the various registers and receivers in the early part of last summer it was perceived that the receipts arising from the sales of the public lands were increasing to an unprecedented amount. In effect, however, these receipts amounted to nothing more than credits in bank. The banks lent out their notes to speculators. They were paid to the receivers and immediately returned to the banks, to be lent out again and again, being mere instruments to transfer to speculators the most valuable public land and pay the Government by a credit on the books of the banks. Those credits on the books of some of the Western banks, usually called deposits, were already greatly beyond their immediate means of payment, and were rapidly increasing. Indeed, each speculation furnished means for another; for no sooner had one individual or company paid in the notes than they were immediately lent to another for a like purpose, and the banks were extending their business and their issues so largely as to alarm considerate men and render it doubtful whether these bank credits if permitted to accumulate would ultimately be of the least value to the Government. The spirit of expansion and speculation was not confined to the deposit banks, but pervaded the whole multitude of banks throughout the Union and was giving rise to new institutions to aggravate the evil.

The safety of the public funds and the interest of the people generally required that these operations should be checked; and it became the duty of every branch of the General and State Governments to adopt all legitimate and proper means to produce that salutary effect. Under this view of my duty I directed the issuing of the order which will be laid before you by the Secretary of the Treasury, requiring payment for the public lands sold to be made in specie, with an exception until the 15th of the present month in favor of actual settlers. This measure has produced many salutary consequences. It checked the career of the Western banks and gave them additional strength in anticipation of the pressure which has since pervaded our Eastern as well as the European commercial cities. By preventing the extension of the credit system it measurably cut off the means of speculation and retarded its progress in monopolizing the most valuable of the public lands. It has tended to save the new States from a nonresident proprietorship, one of the greatest obstacles to the advancement of a new country and the prosperity of an old one. It has tended to keep open the public lands for entry by emigrants at Government prices instead of their being compelled to purchase of speculators at double or triple prices. And it is conveying into the interior large sums in silver and gold, there to enter permanently into the currency of the country and place it on a firmer foundation. It is confidently believed that the country will find in the motives which induced that order and the happy consequences which will have ensued much to commend and nothing to condemn.

It remains for Congress if they approve the policy which dictated this order to follow it up in its various bearings. Much good, in my judgment, would be produced by prohibiting sales of the public lands except to actual settlers at a reasonable reduction of price, and to limit the quantity which shall be sold to them. Although it is believed the General Government never ought to receive anything but the constitutional currency in exchange for the public lands, that point would be of less importance if the lands were sold for immediate settlement and cultivation. Indeed, there is scarcely a mischief arising out of our present land system, including the accumulating surplus of revenues, which would not be remedied at once by a restriction on land sales to actual settlers; and it promises other advantages to the country in general and to the new States in particular which can not fail to receive the most profound consideration of Congress. . . .

The lessons taught by the Bank of the United States can not well be lost upon the American people. They will take care never again to place so tremendous a power in irresponsible hands, and it will be fortunate if they seriously consider the consequences which are likely to result on a small scale from the facility with which corporate powers are granted by their State governments. . . .

The military movements rendered necessary by the aggressions of the hostile portions of the Seminole and Creek tribes of Indians, and by other circumstances, have required the active employment of nearly our whole regular force, including the Marine Corps, and of large bodies of militia and volunteers. . . .

The national policy, founded alike in interest and in humanity, so long and so steadily pursued by this Government for the removal of the Indian tribes originally settled on this side of the Mississippi to the west of that river, may be said to have been consummated by the conclusion of the late treaty with the Cherokees. . . .

All my experience and reflection confirm the conviction I have so often expressed to Congress in favor of an amendment of the Constitution which will prevent in any event the election of the President and Vice-President of the United States devolving on the House of Representatives and the Senate, and I therefore beg leave again to solicit your attention to the subject. . . .

Having now finished the observations deemed proper on this the last occasion I shall have of communicating with the two Houses of Congress at their meeting, I can not omit an expression of the gratitude which is due to the great body of my fellow-citizens, in whose partiality and indulgence I have found encouragement and support in the many difficult and trying scenes through which it has been my lot to pass during my public career. Though deeply sensible that my exertions have not been crowned with a success corresponding to the degree of favor bestowed upon me, I am sure that they will be considered as having been directed by an earnest desire to promote the good of my country, and I am consoled by the persuasion that whatever errors have been committed will find a corrective in the intelligence and patriotism of those who will succeed us. All that has occurred during my Administration is calculated to inspire me with increased confidence in the stability of our institutions; and should I be spared to enter upon that retirement which is so suitable to my age and infirm health and so much desired by me in other respects, I shall not cease to invoke that beneficent Being to whose providence we are already so signally indebted for the continuance of His blessings on our beloved country.

ANDREW JACKSON.

JACKSON'S MESSAGES ON TEXAS
December 21, 1836
March 3, 1837

*Although Jackson was an expansionist who earlier
had sought to purchase Texas from Mexico, when
Texas declared its independence Jackson delayed recognition of the Republic of Texas until the last day
of his administrations.*

Washington, December 21, 1836

To the Senate and House of Representatives of the United States:

During the last session information was given to Congress by the
Executive that measures had been taken to ascertain "the political,
military, and civil condition of Texas.". . . .

No steps have been taken by the Executive toward the acknowledgment of the independence of Texas, and the whole subject would have
been left without further remark on the information now given to
Congress were it not that the two Houses at their last session, acting
separately, passed resolutions "that the independence of Texas ought
to be acknowledged by the United States whenever satisfactory information should be received that it had in successful operation a
civil government capable of performing the duties and fulfilling the
obligations of an independent power." This mark of interest in the
question of the independence of Texas and indication of the views
of Congress make it proper that I should somewhat in detail present
the considerations that have governed the Executive in continuing to
occupy the ground previously taken in the contest between Mexico
and Texas.

The acknowledgment of a new state as independent and entitled to
a place in the family of nations is at all times an act of great delicacy and responsibility, but more especially so when such state has
forcibly separated itself from another of which it had formed an in-
tegral part and which still claims dominion over it. A premature
recognition under these circumstances, if not looked upon as jus-
tifiable cause of war, is always liable to be regarded as a proof of
an unfriendly spirit to one of the contending parties. . . .

It has thus been made known to the world that the uniform policy
and practice of the United States is to avoid all interference in dis-
putes which merely relate to the internal government of other nations,
and eventually to recognize the authority of the prevailing party,
without reference to our particular interests and views or to the merits
of the original controversy. . . .

It is true that, with regard to Texas, the civil authority of Mexico has been expelled, its invading army defeated, the chief of the Republic himself captured, and all present power to control the newly organized Government of Texas annihilated within its confines. But, on the other hand, there is, in appearance at least, an immense disparity of physical force on the side of Mexico. The Mexican Republic under another executive is rallying its forces under a new leader and menacing a fresh invasion to recover its lost dominion.

Upon the issue of this threatened invasion the independence of Texas may be considered as suspended, and were there nothing peculiar in the relative situation of the United States and Texas our acknowledgment of its independence at such a crisis would scarcely be regarded as consistent with that prudent reserve with which we have heretofore held ourselves bound to treat all similar questions. But there are circumstances in the relations of the two countries which require us to act on the occasion with even more than our wonted caution. Texas was once claimed as a part of our property, and there are those among our citizens who, always reluctant to abandon that claim, can not but regard with solicitude the prospect of the reunion of the territory to this country. A large proportion of its civilized inhabitants are emigrants from the United States, speak the same language with ourselves, cherish the same principles, political and religious, and are bound to many of our citizens by ties of friendship and kindred blood; and, more than all, it is known that the people of that country have instituted the same form of government with our own, and have since the close of your last session openly resolved, on the acknowledgment by us of their independence, to seek admission into the Union as one of the Federal States. This last circumstance is a matter of peculiar delicacy, and forces upon us considerations of the gravest character. The title of Texas to the territory she claims is identified with her independence. She asks us to acknowledge that title to the territory, with an avowed design to treat immediately of its transfer to the United States. It becomes us to beware of a too early movement, as it might subject us, however unjustly, to the imputation of seeking to establish the claim of our neighbors to a territory with a view to its subsequent acquistion by ourselves. Prudence, therefore, seems to dictate that we should still stand aloof and maintain our present attitude, if not until Mexico itself or one of the great foreign powers shall recognize the independence of the new Government, at least until the lapse of time or the course of events shall have proved beyond cavil or dispute the ability of the people of that country to maintain their separate sovereignty and to uphold the Government constituted by them. Neither of the contending parties can justly complain of this course. By pursuing it we are but carrying out the long-established policy of our Government—a policy which has secured to us respect and influence abroad and inspired confidence at home. ...

ANDREW JACKSON.

Washington, March 3, 1837

To the Senate of the United States:

In my message to Congress of the 21st of December last I laid before that body, without reserve, my views concerning the recognition of the independence of Texas, with a report of the agent employed by the Executive to obtain information in respect to the condition of that country. Since that time the subject has been repeatedly discussed in both branches of the Legislature. These discussions have resulted in the insertion of a clause in the general appropriation law passed by both Houses providing for the outfit and salary of a diplomatic agent to be sent to the Republic of Texas whenever the President of the United States may receive satisfactory evidence that Texas is an independent power and shall deem it expedient to appoint such minister, and in the adoption of a resolution by the Senate, the constitutional advisers of the Executive on the diplomatic intercourse of the United States with foreign powers, expressing the opinion that "the State of Texas having established and maintained an independent government capable of performing those duties, foreign and domestic, which appertain to independent governments, and it appearing that there is no longer any reasonable prospect of the successful prosecution of the war by Mexico against said State, it is expedient and proper and in conformity with the laws of nations and the practice of this Government in like cases that the independent political existence of said State be acknowledged by the Government of the United States." Regarding these proceedings as a virtual decision of the question submitted by me to Congress, I think it my duty to acquiesce therein, and therefore I nominate Alcée La Branche, of Louisiana, to be chargé d'affaires to the Republic of Texas.

ANDREW JACKSON.

Bibliographical Aids

The emphasis in this and subsequent volumes in the *Presidential Chronologies* series will be on the administrations of the Presidents. The more important works on other aspects of their lives, either before or after their terms, are included since they may contribute to an understanding of the presidential careers.

The following bibliography is critically selected. Many additional titles may be found in the works by Van Deusen, Remini, and Schlesinger listed below and in the standard guides. The student might also wish to consult *Reader's Guide to Periodical Literature* and *Social Sciences and Humanities Index* (formerly *International Index)* for recent articles in scholarly journals.

Additional chronological information not included in this volume because it did not relate directly to the president, may be found in the *Encyclopedia of American History,* edited by Richard B. Morris revised edition (New York, 1965).

Asterisks after titles refer to books currently available in paperback editions.

SOURCE MATERIALS

The papers that Jackson himself preserved so carefully in order that they might be used for a full account of his life were not kept intact by those who later came into possession of them. A brief account of the disposition of these papers can be found in the preface to the biography by John Spencer Bassett (see Biographies below). The basic printed source for Jackson's letters is John Spencer Bassett, ed., *Correspondence of Andrew Jackson,* 7 vols. (Washington, 1926-35). Most of the MSS themselves are in the "Montgomery Blair Collection" in the Library of Congress, known as the "Jackson MSS." Lesser collections of Jackson letters are in the New York Public Library (Major William B. Lewis Papers), the Tennessee Historical Society (Dyas Collection) and in the Andrew Jackson Donelson Papers in the Library of Congress. Jackson kept no diary. For source materials relating to other leaders in the Jacksonian era see the Bibliographic Essay in Glyndon G. Van Deusen, *The Jacksonian Era* (New York, 1959). Three sources available in most libraries are listed below:

Blau, Joseph L., ed. *Social Theories of Jacksonian Democracy: Repre-sentative Writings of the Period 1825-1850.* New York, 1954. Selec-tions by Jacksonian writers on self-government, economic themes, and social criticism.

Eaton, Clement, ed. *The Leaven of Democracy: The Growth of the Democratic Spirit in the Time of Jackson.* New York, 1963.* Con-temporary views of Jacksonian politics and society organized by geographical region, with excellent introductions by the editor.

Syrett, Harold C. *Andrew Jackson: His Contribution to the American Tradition.* Indianapolis, 1953. After a brief chronology and intro-duction, includes many letters and other documents on Jackson and his times.

BIOGRAPHIES

Bassett, John Spencer. *The Life of Andrew Jackson.* 2 vols. in one. New York, 1910 (second edition, 1915). One of the best biogra-phies of Jackson, the first to make thorough use of Jackson's papers and those of his associates. Basset reflected the reform spirit of the Progressive Era, emphasizing Jackson's democratic leadership.

James, Marquis. *Andrew Jackson: The Border Captain.* Indianapolis, 1933. The first of the two volume biography of Jackson written by a distinguished journalist who died in 1955. An introduction to Jackson, the man, covering his early life in the Waxhaws and in North Carolina and Tennessee, and his military leadership at New Orleans and in Florida.

James, Marquis. *Andrew Jackson: Portrait of a President.* Indiana-polis, 1937. The best account of Jackson's personal and family life in the presidency; a portrait rather than a political history written in a moving style.

Parton, James L. *The Life of Andrew Jackson.* 3 vols. New York, 1859-1860. Written only fifteen years after Jackson's death, this biography used the personal reminiscences of participants in his administration, particularly Major William B. Lewis. Parton wrote from the viewpoint of the eastern patrician, charged Jackson with the creation of the Spoils System, and concluded that more harm than good came from his election.

Remini, Robert V. *Andrew Jackson.* New York, 1966. The best brief biography of Andrew Jackson, written in a lively style, sympa-thetic to Jackson, emphasizing his political leadership. Both scholarly and readable, this is the place to begin for the student of Jacksonian Democracy.

Sumer, William Graham. *Andrew Jackson As A Public Man: What He Was, What Chances He Had, and What He Did With Them.* Boston, 1882. A good nineteenth century biography of Jackson.

Johnson, Gerald W. *Andrew Jackson: An Epic in Homespun.* New York, 1927. Well-written, sympathetic to Jackson, but less than a third of the volume deals with Jackson's presidency.

ESSAYS

The student should consult the articles on Jackson in encyclopedias and collections such as those by Thomas P. Abernethy in the *Dictionary of American Biography,* Harold W. Bradley in the *Encyclopedia Brittanica* and Richard A. McLemore in the *Encyclopedia Americana.* Other essays include the following:

Abernethy, Thomas P. "Andrew Jackson and the Rise of Southwestern Democracy,*"American Historical Review,*XXXIII (October, 1927), 64-77.

Chambers, William N. "Andrew Jackson" in *America's Ten Greatest Presidents* edited by Morton Borden (Chicago, 1961), 81-112.*

Dorfman, Joseph. "The Jackson Wage-Earner Thesis," *American Historical Review,* LIV (January, 1949), 296-306.

Gatell, Frank Otto. "Money and Party in Jacksonian America: A Quantitative Look at New York City's Men of Quality," *Political Science Quarterly,* LXXXII (June, 1967), 235-252.

Hammond, Bray. "Jackson, Biddle, and the Bank of the United States," *Journal of Economic History,* VII (May, 1947), 1-23.

Hofstadter, Richard. "Andrew Jackson and the Rise of Liberal Capitalism," chapter III in *The American Political Tradition and the Men Who Made It* (New York, 1948).*

Lebowitz, Michael A. "The Jacksonians: Paradox Lost?" chapter III in *Towards a New Past: Dissenting Essays in American History,* edited by Barton J. Bernstein (New York, 1968).

Longaker, Richard P. "Was Jackson's Kitchen Cabinet a Cabinet?" *Mississippi Valley Historical Review,* XLVI (June, 1957), 94-108.

McCormick, Richard P. "New Perspectives on Jacksonian Politics," *American Historical Review.* LXV (January, 1960), 288-301.

Marshall, Lynn. "The Authorship of Jackson's Bank Veto Message," *Mississippi Valley Historical Review*, L (December, 1963), 466-477.

Morris, Richard B. "Andrew Jackson, Strikebreaker," *American Historical Review*, LV (October, 1949), 54-68.

Pessen, Edward. "The Working Men's Movement of the Jacksonian Era," *Mississippi Valley Historical Review*, XLIII (December, 1956), 428-443.

Sellers, Charles G. "Andrew Jackson versus the Historians," *Mississippi Valley Historical Review*, XLIV (March, 1958), 615-634.

Sullivan, William A. "Did Labor Support Andrew Jackson?" *Political Science Quarterly*, LXII (December, 1947), 579-580.

Van Deusen, Glyndon G. "Some Aspects of Whig Thought and Theory in The Jacksonian Period," *American Historical Review*, LXIII (January, 1958), 305-322.

Ward, John William. "The Age of the Common Man" chapter 5 in *The Reconstruction of American History*, edited by John Higham (New York, 1962).*

MONOGRAPHS AND SPECIAL AREAS

Abernethy, Thomas P. *From Frontier to Plantation in Tennessee: A Study in Frontier Democracy*. Memphis, 1955. Shows Jackson opposed to the democratic reform movement in Tennessee rather than its leader before he entered the presidency and challenges the Frontier Thesis of Frederick Jackson Turner.

Benson, Lee. *The Concept of Jacksonian Democracy: New York as a Test Case*. Princeton, 1961. Making close analysis of New York voting returns, Benson discards the concept of Jacksonian Democracy, particularly in its economic origins, and proposes instead an egalitarian interpretation of the age in which Jackson was President.

Beveridge, Albert J. *The Life of John Marshall*. 4 vols. Boston, 1919. Volume IV of this classic biography covers the judicial history of the Jacksonian period.

Catterall, Ralph C. H. *The Second Bank of the United States*. Chicago, 1903. Still basic for study of this institution.

Filler, Louis and Guttman, Allen, eds. *The Removal of the Cherokee Nation: Manifest Destiny or National Dishonor* Boston, 1962.

Problems in American Civilization, edited by *George Rogers Taylor.** Presents a broad range of judgments on Jackson's Indian removal policy, including views of contemporary participants and more recent historians.

Foreman, Grant. *Indian Removal: The Emigration of the Five Civilized Tribes of Indians.* Norman, 1932. Describes the human suffering, sorrow, and tragedy of the Indian removal under Jackson's administrations, contrasting with the favorable reports in his annual messages.

Hammond, Bray. *Banks and Politics in America: From the Revolution to the Civil War.* 2 vols. Princeton, 1957*. Second volume includes Jackson's "war on the bank." The class-conflict approach to this issue is sharply challenged as Hammond finds the Jacksonians not opposed to all banks in a struggle between the rich and the poor, but rather seeking to gain equality of opportunity for state banks and new entrepreneurs who were fearful of government sponsored monopoly.

Handlin, Oscar and Mary F. *Commonwealth: A Study of the Role of Government in the American Economy: Massachusetts, 1744-1861.* Cambridge, 1947.

Hartz, Louis. *Economic Policy and Democratic Thought: Pennsylvania, 1776-1860.* Cambridge, 1948.

Hartz, Louis. *The Liberal Tradition in America: An Interpretation of American Political Thought Since the Revolution.* New York, 1955. A comparative approach to the Jacksonian era showing confusion and paradox in the liberalism of the farmer and the laborer as they opposed a capitalist aristocracy.

Heath, Milton S. *Constructive Liberalism: The Role of the State in Economic Development in Georgia to 1860.* Cambridge, 1954.

Hoffman, William S. *Andrew Jackson and North Carolina Politics.* Chapel Hill, 1958.

Hugins, Walter. *Jacksonian Democracy and the Working Class: A Study of the New York Workingmen's Movement 1829-1837.* Stanford, 1960. Extends the entrepreneurial interpretation of Jacksonian Democracy to include New York Workingmen, finding them not so much opposed to American capitalism as desiring equal opportunity to rise within it.

Miller, Douglas T. *Jacksonian Aristocracy: Class and Democracy in New York, 1830-1860.* New York, 1967.

Primm, James N. *Economic Policy in the Development of a Western State: Missouri, 1820-1860.* Cambridge, 1954.

Pessen, Edward. *Most Uncommon Jacksonians: The Radical Leaders of the Early Labor Movement.* Albany, 1967. An authoritative study of the workers of the Jacksonian era and their leaders in the Working Men's parties, describing their radical attacks on the conditions of American society and their opposition to both Whigs and Jacksonian Democrats.

Remini, Robert V. *Andrew Jackson and the Bank War: A Study of the Growth of Presidental Power.* New York, 1967. A political study of the crucial controversy of Jacksons administrations. Engagingly written and particularly valuable as it traces the conflict "between two willful, proud, and stubborn men: Andrew Jackson and Nicholas Biddle."

Remini, Robert V. *The Election of Andrew Jackson.* Philadelphia, 1963.* A vivid account of Jacksons triumph over John Quincy Adams in 1828. His victory is attributed to his enormous popularity and especially to the remarkable growth of party organization. Issues were unclear but Jackson's supporters worked for a "political revolution."

Remini, Robert V. *Martin Van Buren and the Making of the Democratic Party.* New York, 1959. Shows the work of Van Buren in the organization of the Democratic Party before Jackson's election to the presidency.

Shaw, Ronald E. *Erie Water West: A History of the Erie Canal 1792-1854.* Lexington, 1966. Includes a study of the conflict between Jacksonians and Whigs in New York over canals.

Smith, Walter B. *Economic Aspects of the Second Bank of the United States.* Cambridge, 1953.

Stevens, Harry R. *The Early Jackson Party in Ohio.* Durham, 1957.

Thompson, Arthur W. *Jacksonian Democracy on the Florida Frontier.* Gainesville, 1961.

Tocqueville, Alexis de. *Democracy in America.* 2 vols., edited by Phillips Bradley. New York, 1945.* A classic view of American society and institutions in the Jacksonian period by a perceptive French traveler.

JACKSONIAN DEMOCRACY

Alexander, Holmes. *The American Talleyrand: The Career and Contemporaries of Martin Van Buren, Eighth President.* New York, 1935. Critical of Van Buren's contributions to Jacksonian Democracy.

Bowers, Claude G. *The Party Battles of the Jackson Period.* Boston, 1922. Highly partisan in support of Jackson but conveys the spirit of Jacksonian politics. For a briefer statement of this approach, likely to attract the student's interest, see the chapter on Jackson in this author's *Making Democracy a Reality: Jefferson, Jackson, and Polk* (Memphis, 1954).

Bugg, James L., ed. *Jacksonian Democracy: Myth or Reality.* New York, 1963. *American Problem Studies* edited by Oscar Handlin.* Groups the interpretations of Jacksonian Democracy into the "Patrician School," "Democratic School," "New Critical School," "Class Conflict School," "Entreprenurial School," and "School of Symbolism and Psychology."

Cave, Alfred A. *Jacksonian Democracy and the Historians.* Gainesville, 1964.* One of the best surveys of historical literature on Jacksonian Democracy.

Coit, Margaret L. *John C. Calhoun, American Patriot.* Boston, 1950.* Includes detailed treatment of Calhoun's personal and family life, almost eulogistic in tone.

Current, Richard. *Daniel Webster and the Rise of National Conservatism.* Boston, 1955.* Brief but scholarly account of Jackson's famous New England opponent.

Eaton, Clement. *Henry Clay and the Art of American Politics.* Boston, 1957.* Brief but scholarly account of a major figure in the Jacksonian era.

Fish, Carl Russell. *The Rise of the Common Man, 1830-1850.* New York, 1927. An early social history emphasizing the frontier influence on Jacksonian Democracy.

Govan, Thomas. *Nicholas Biddle: Nationalist and Public Banker, 1786-1844.* Chicago, 1959. Gives the viewpoint of Jackson's chief antagonist in the Bank War.

Lynch, Denis T. *An Epoch and a Man, Martin Van Buren and His Times.* New York, 1929. Emphasizes Van Buren's achievements in the Jacksonian era.

McCormick, Richard P. *The Second American Party system: Party Formation in the Jacksonian Era.* Chapel Hill, 1966. A state by state analysis of the formation of the Democratic and Whig parties in the years between 1824 and 1840 stressing the distinctive elements of this "second party system" rather than continuity with other periods of party history.

MacDonald, William. *Jacksonian Democracy.* New York, 1906. A volume in the first American Nation Series, edited by A. B. Hart, significant in identifying Jackson with a period of Democratic reform.

Meyers, Marvin. *The Jacksonian Persuasion: Politics and Belief.* Palo Alto (Cal.), 1957* A symbolic approach to Jacksonian Democracy showing its attempts to preserve the older virtues of Republican simplicity associated with Jeffersonian America while new economic interests were leading America toward acquisition, speculation, and industry.

Pessen, Edward. *Jacksonian America: Society, Personality, and Politics.* Homewood, 1969.* An excellent comprehensive study of the Jacksonian era.

Riegel, Robert E. *Young America, 1830-1840.* Norman (Okla.), 1949. A good social history of the United States in the period of Jacksonian Democracy.

Rozwenc, Edwin C., ed. *The Meaning of Jacksonian Democracy.* Boston, 1963. *Problems in American Civilization* edited by George Rogers Taylor.* Includes views of the Jacksonians by contemporary leaders, European observers and twentieth century historians.

Schlesinger, Arthur M. Jr. *The Age of Jackson.* Boston, 1945.* Pulitzer Prize winning study which interprets Jacksonian Democracy as supported by eastern workingmen and intellectuals as well as frontier farmers.

Turner, Frederick Jackson. *The United States, 1830-1850: The Nation and its Sections.* New York, 1935. Chapter IX relates political issues of Jackson's administrations to sectional developments, and illustrates this author's famous Frontier Thesis.

Tyler, Alice Felt. *Freedom's Ferment: Phases of American Social History from the Colonial Period to the Outbreak of the Civil War.* New York, 1944.* Includes excellent account of social reforms in the Jacksonian era.

Van Deusen, Glyndon B. *The Jacksonian Era, 1828-1848.* New York, 1959.* The basic political history of the Jacksonians and Whigs in the period from the election of 1828 to the end of the Mexican War. Unravels the complex political relationships in the issues of the tariff and the bank and traces emergence of the "New Jacksonians" who supported James K. Polk.

Ward, John William. *Andrew Jackson: Symbol for an Age.* New York, 1955.* Using the newer approaches of psychology to history, this study shows Jackson reflecting rather than shaping the dominant ideals of his age. Finds three central concepts in American virtues, Nature, Providence and Will, realized in Andrew Jackson. Like Remini's biography this relatively small volume is an excellent place to start for the student of Jacksonian Democracy.

White, Leonard D. *The Jacksonians: A Study in Administrative History 1829-1861.* New York, 1954.* A detailed source for the student investigating topics such as the presidency, the Cabinet, Congress, the courts or the military services during the Jacksonian era. The author has made similar studies in public administration for the Federalists, Jeffersonians, and Republicans.

Wiltse, Charles M. *John C. Calhoun: Nullifier, 1829-1839.* Indianapolis, 1949. Second volume of the definitive biography of Calhoun, elevates Calhoun at the expense of Jackson.

THE PRESIDENCY

Bailey, Thomas A. *Presidential Greatness: The Image and the Man from George Washington to the Present.* New York, 1966.* A critical and subjective study of the qualities of presidential greatness, arranged topically rather than chronologically. Bailey lists forty-three yardsticks for measuring presidential ability, disagrees with the ranking given Jackson in the Schlesinger polls of "Great" or first among the "Near Great" and instead rates him as "not better than high Average, if that." The book includes an excellent up to date bibliography on presidential powers and problems, with special emphasis on measuring effectiveness or greatness according to the Bailey criteria.

Binkley, Wilfred E. *The Man in the White House: His Powers and Duties.* Revised ed. New York, 1964. Treats the development of the various roles of the American president.

Brown, Stuart Gerry. *The American Presidency: Leadership, Partisanship, and Popularity.* New York, 1966. Seems to like the more partisan presidents such as Jefferson and Jackson.

Burns, James MacGregor. *Presidential Government: The Crucible of Leadership.* New York, 1966.*

Corwin, Edward S. *The President: Office and Powers.* 4th revised ed. New York, 1957.* An older classic.

Cunliffe, Marcus. *The American Heritage History of the Presidency.* New York, 1968. A recent interpretation by a competent authority.

Haight, David E. & Johnston, Larry D. *The President: Roles and Powers.* Chicago, 1965.* Essays on the presidency by both Presidents and other experts.

Israel, Fred L., ed. *The State of the Union Messages of the Presidents. 1790-1966.* New York, 1967. Contains introduction by Arthur M. Schlesinger, Jr.

Kane, Joseph Nathan. *Facts about the Presidents.* Revised ed. New York, 1968.* Useful, with complete information on the President's family, nominating conventions, and cabinet appointments. Includes comparative as well as biographical data about the Presidents.

Koenig, Louis W. *The Chief Executive.* New York, 1964. Authoritative study of presidential powers.

Laski, Harold J. *The American Presidency.* New York, 1940.* A classic.

Roseboom, Eugene H. *A History of Presidential Elections.* Revised ed. New York, 1964.

Rossiter, Clinton. *The American Presidency.* 2nd ed. New York, 1960.* A standard treatment by an outstanding authority.

NAME INDEX

TITLES IN THE OCEANA
PRESIDENTIAL CHRONOLOGY SERIES

Reference books containing Chronology — Documents — Bibliographical Aids for each President covered.

Series Editor: Howard F. Bremer

   *   96 pages, $3.00/B, available now.
  ** 128 pages, $4.00/B, available now.
*** 160 pages, $5.00/B, available late 1969.